THE SOCIAL ECONOMY OF FRANCE

The Social Economy of France

1928419

PETER COFFEY

Senior Fellow in European Economics
Europa Instituut, University of Amsterdam

MACMILLAN

First published 1973 by
THE MACMILLAN PRESS LTD
London and Basingstoke
Associated companies in New York Dublin
Melbourne Johannesburg and Madras

SBN 333 13758 2

Printed in Great Britain by
R. AND R. CLARK LTD
Edinburgh

A /309. /44

Pour Bernard, Jean-Pierre et Madame Jouanneau

Intacte, énorme, éternelle . . . voilà de grands adjectifs, et qui sentent la considération, tout au moins celle qu'on doit à une puissance.

Colette, *Le Pur et l'impur*

Pour la technique, je m'en tenais à l'objectivité que je m'imposais . . . m'interdisant de jamais faire comprendre un personnage par une description introspective; mais seulement, comme dans la vie, par ce qu'on peut voir ou entendre: leurs gestes, les mains qui les trahissent, les paroles toujours chargées d'ambiguïté, les silences qui les mettent à nu sans qu'ils s'en doutent.

Vercors, *La Bataille du silence*

CONTENTS

Effects of the French Taxation System: French
Banking Reforms

List of Tables

Unless otherwise indicated, all the statistics in this book are from the I.N.S.E.E.

Preface: Why Study France?

During the 1950s and the 1960s, it was fashionable to study the economy of France because France had applied a system of indicative planning in a most successful manner. By the middle 1960s, due partly to the opening up of France to her neighbours in the European Economic Community, partly to the influx of refugees from Algeria and partly to her desire to make the franc a 'hard' currency, the attitude to both national planning and to economic management in general changed. Together with this change of attitude, after the 'May Events' of 1968, two fundamental changes in the structure of the French economy became more evident – changes which were not directly results of these upheavals. One of these changes was a greater concern with social policy than had hitherto been the case (at least greater than at any time since the period 1944–8). In a way, this change was accelerated by the unheavals of May 1968. The other change which became obvious by 1970, which is very important because it is a condition which France had not known for several decades, is the emergence of large-scale unemployment. It is this latter development and the measures which France is using to tackle the attendant problems which would make any study of the French economy worthwhile.

The current attention to social policy is worthy of our interest both by the sheer novelty of some of the measures used and by the order of priorities which the French have chosen. In this field, the very nature of the problems which France is trying to solve and their similarity with those in other countries are worthy of study.

Apart from the analysis of the problems and the measures used to solve them, the description of the different social and economic organisations and groups in France, and the account of the management of the French national economy, the real aim has been to attempt to draw some basic qualitative and quantitative conclusions regarding the standard of living in France. Just as Britain becomes a full member of the enlarged

European Economic Community, it is useful that we should attempt to gauge the standard of living in our neighbours' countries and it is equally important that we assess the health and future evolution of those economies with which we are conducting an important part of our trade.

Most studies concerned with the standard of living in individual countries have difficulty in finding a measuring rod for this purpose. Too frequently we are assailed with the barrage of statistics which normally indicates the numbers of cars and refrigerators in a particular country. But if in such a country there are so many cars on the roads that one cannot move, if the food is mediocre and the quality of clothes poor, and if in order to obtain the cars and refrigerators one must forego all free time, then one might conclude that the standard of living is very bad indeed! Equally, it is extremely difficult to rely on subjective criteria – if one likes lots of reasonably priced wine and acres of untouched countryside – then France would be extremely attractive. In practice however, we do know that direct taxes are relatively low, that family allowances are good, that professional salaries tend to be high, that there is a great expansion in the service industries, that holidays are many and long, and that there is little prejudice against women occupying important professional positions. Thus if one were married and both partners were professionally employed, and if one had a number of children, then France would be an extremely attractive country in which to live. If on the other hand, one wishes to buy a large house near to a major urban centre and to send one's children to University, if one were not earning a large salary, one should settle down in Britain! Nevertheless, as is the case in Britain for qualities peculiar to our own country, France still has certain qualities unique to herself – her food (though generally less excellent than a decade ago) is still good and varied, her intellectual life is still very stimulating, and though Britain may still have the stronger public institutions, in France personal friendships and relationships tend to be very excellent.

Further Social and Economic Considerations

In the socio-economic sphere this is indeed an exciting moment to study France. Everything seems to be changing and everything is being questioned. At the time of writing, the best finalists of the *Promotion Charles de Gaulle* at the famous *Ecole Nationale d'Administration* have refused to take the first choice of plum jobs in the leading ministries, such as the Ministry of Finance. Instead they have preferred to choose ministries enabling them to have closer contact with the provinces. According to the mood of the next *Promotion-Rabelais*, the same thing will be repeated next year.

As will be noted later in this work, contraception, forbidden since 1920, and in principle reinstated in 1969, has only in December of this year been finally legalised.

In January of this year the prisoners in the dreadful prison at Nancy revolted and their action shook the national conscience. Since then there have been upheavals at several prisons. It is now likely that the antiquated prisons, like the antiquated laws regarding contraception, will be reformed.

In the more purely economic field regarding labour, agreements were made in the spring of this year allowing older workers to receive up to 80% of their pay if unemployed. In this way it is hoped to open up more places to the younger workers. This move follows the successful introduction in the previous year of making most workers salaried employees.

Much progress has been made in the field of female emancipation. The principle is that women should be allowed to go out to work if they so desire, but that their children should not suffer if they do so. Thus, again this year, a working mother who cannot find a *crèche* for her children is given a daily allowance per child with which to pay a person who will look after the children. Equally, should the mother prefer to stay at home to look after her children and only one person in the family be in receipt of a salary, if this be small, then a special allowance (*Allocation de Salaire Unique*) is given. All this is of course apart from the generous family allowances. In the civil service, mothers who prefer to stay at home receive a percentage of their salary over a number of years without losing any seniority rights.

Again in the economic field, this year, the City of Marseille is making the first public loan – on the stock exchange – ever made by a French city. Again we must not ignore the important creation in 1970 of the *Fonds d'Action Conjoncturelle*. This is a fund to be used for anti-cyclical policy which is currently being used to cut down the level of unemployment. Of greater importance was the creation in 1971 of the I.D.I. (*Institut de Développement Industriel*), an institution very similar to the defunct Industrial Reorganisation Corporation. To date, loans have been given to a few pilot firms.

Finally, a study of France's experience since 1963 with a prices and incomes policy, but especially with a prices policy would be of use and interest to economists. And for readers interested in the quality of life, the recent creation of a number of national parks in France, the *Loi Malraux* which allows whole urban areas to be classed as historic monuments, the current designation of a number of medium-sized towns such as Angoulême for special qualitative and material help from the State, and M. Chalandon's decision this year to give subsidies only to council housing of quality, indicate that France is aware of the terrible judgement passed on her by one of her friends when he wrote: *'La France s'enlaidit'*.[1]

Amsterdam   PETER COFFEY
June 1972

Postscript 1972–1973

Since the manuscript of this work was completed, there have been many developments in the social field in France.

It would thus be inadmissible to allow the publication of this work without making reference to these events since they do reflect some of the profound changes which are currently taking place in French society.

At the social level, the changes deeply concern young people, the medical profession and immigrant workers.

Describing the situation in a few words, one might say that young people in France, like their counterparts in Britain during the past decade, will not accept the hypocrisy which surrounds such areas as sexual education, abortion and contraception. Equally, they question the principle of parental control and military service. But, as one would naturally expect, many

---

[1] H. Koningsberger, *Le Monde* (28 August 1970).

members of the older generation would prefer to maintain the old *bien pensant* type of society – probably because it is more comfortable to do so. In turn, after the publication of the *Fontanet–Marcellin* circular, the immigrant workers are less inclined to accept economic and social injustices than was formerly the case.

Ever since the death of Gabrielle Russier in 1969, one has been aware of the battle which the authorities and parents have been waging (and losing, the author would maintain) to re-impose an outdated moral code on young people. During the period 1972–3, the object of their attack has been an excellent, logical, succinct and harmless little paper on sexual questions, written by Dr Carpentier.[1] This paper was circulated among many schools, and sooner or later it had to be the object of a test case. What had to happen, then, did happen. In the autumn of 1972, Madame Mercier, a teacher in the lycée at Belfort, was taken to court by a parent of one of the pupils for having discussed Dr Carpentier's paper in class. After much upheaval and some demonstrations, Madame Mercier was acquitted. Her case does, however, demonstrate the very delicate position of teachers in France. A further example of the equivocal position of teachers there has been the attempt by certain parents' organisations in 1972 and 1973 to ban some of the works of Boris Vian in the lycées since they consider these to be pornographic.

Possibly of greater importance was the Bobigny court case concerning an abortion carried out on a girl who was under age. This important event led to declarations both written and verbal, by the most illustrious doctors (including Nobel prize winners) in France, supporting their colleague, and to the publication on 7 February 1973 by 206 doctors of a declaration that they had also been parties to abortion.[2]

At parliamentary level, important social laws were passed. In November 1972, a special law was passed to reinforce the equal rights between men and women. Also, a law was passed regarding the dismissal of workers, which placed the responsibility for the proof of incompetence on the employer.

In December 1972, after several years of procrastination, the

---

[1] *Apprenons à faire l'Amour.*

[2] A similar affair erupted in Grenoble in May 1973 as a result of the prosecution of Dr Ferrey-Martin.

Law Neuwirth was finally passed in its complete form, thus finally legalising contraception and establishing State aid for the creation of family planning centres in France.

The reaction of those in authority has been amply demonstrated by the menacing tone adopted at the Congress of the Paris police trade union, held in May 1973, when newspapers and progressive judges were bitterly criticised.

Mention has been made of the immigrant workers. It is probably the main gap in this book. Apart from the statistics devoted to the numbers of these workers, attention has not been, unfortunately, paid to the grave injustices which many of these workers face in France – as they do in other countries. Basically speaking, the problem in France is threefold. Firstly, the economic boom there is such that enormous numbers of labourers and industrial workers are needed to enable it to continue. Secondly, because of the need to import workers, many employers are willing to collaborate with the movement of large numbers of clandestine workers into France (about half the foreign workers now entering France do so illegally) with all the disastrous consequences for living conditions and basic rights which this entails for these workers. Thirdly and lastly, the resources at the disposal of the Office National d'Immigration (created in 1945 to adopt a more liberal and helpful attitude towards immigrant workers) are quite inadequate for the task which this organisation has to face. The publication of the *Fontanet–Marcellin* Circular concerning the basic rights of immigrant workers led to a number of hunger strikes by these workers throughout France – often supported by French workers and their unions. However, until adequate resources are given for the housing and education of immigrant workers and their children, and until employers cease to collaborate with the illegal immigration of workers, and until (as is the problem in other countries in Europe) Frenchmen more readily accept these workers in the human and social sense, it is difficult to see how the lot of these people will improve.

Of a more optimistic nature was the agreement made in January 1973 between the *Régie Renault* and the unions to introduce an early form of retirement for their workers at the age of 62.

At the purely economic level, France resorted to the use of a new weapon and to the use of three old weapons, in an attempt to curb the inflation which has beset her like the rest of Western Europe. The new and really imaginative move took the form of cuts in the V.A.T. Many economists fear that the effects of this move will be shortlived. However, resorting to more well-tried policies, France, at the turn of the year 1972–73, placed curbs on bank lending (which have just been successful), launched a very successful State loan, and decided (in the face of opposition from the employers' federation) to continue the price controls which had been introduced on 1 April 1972.

France then, in her move into the twenty-first century, is experiencing deep economic and social changes. Alas, when one looks at the scarred face of the country – the sacrilege committed already on the right bank of the Seine and now to be committed on the left bank,[1] when one looks at the devastation of the Côte d'Azur[2] and other provinces . . . all for the sake of the worship of profit, one wonders whether the current human reactions to the state of French society are not already too late. It will unfortunately take decades to effect the necessary transformation in France in the fields of decentralisation, town planning, education in modern architecture, civic consciousness and active participation at all levels of society. The task before France is indeed monumental. The author, like all who love France, hopes that she will succeed in this task; it is important for the rest of Europe that she succeed.

Amsterdam   PETER COFFEY
May 1973

[1] President Pompidou himself has indeed declared that Paris must be adapted to the automobile!

[2] The State has actively tried to suppress the *Rapport Lamoureux*, consecrated to the protection of the Côte d'Azur, and which also revealed the grave financial corruption encountered in speculative building operations at Bormes-les-Mimosas.

1 Social Philosophy

Few countries in the world have placed philosophy on so elevated a pedestal as has France. Few countries in the world initiate most of their schoolchildren in philosophy and teach them to think; and very few countries exhibit so many different currents of thinking, whether it be in economics, in politics or in the social field. It is this very wealth of thinking that makes this section a difficult one to tackle; a task rendered even more difficult by the near impossibility of attempting to divorce this section of the work from the next one, which is devoted to external affairs. This difficulty is enhanced by the fact that France was technically at war between 1939 and 1962, which in turn meant an acute accentuation of the politicisation between different groups in the country and their schools of thought. Equally the postwar pursuit of military objectives reduced the resources which might have been devoted to certain social ends, thus in turn accentuating the politicisation in the country.

Perhaps this section should begin with a brief look at the legacy that the First World War had bequeathed to France. The legacy took the form of a much reduced population. The quantitative reduction in the size of the population might not have been so serious had it not been also a qualitative one.[1] Quite simply France had lost the flower of her youth during that conflict (1,400,000 men – mostly young). This was to have very grave consequences for her political life, since politics inevitably became a pursuit for old men – with the calamitous results we were to witness in the late 1930s. In a slightly different social sphere, the reduced size of the population led to an obsession with increasing the birth-rate (contraception was outlawed in 1920, and only very lightly freed in 1969).[2] This in turn meant that social welfare policy was to be devoted very much to family allowances – an interest shared by socialists, gaullistes and members of the Vichy régime alike, and only to abate with

[1] The question of population is dealt with in some depth in Chapter 3.
[2] Finally completely legalised in December 1972.

the fall from power of de Gaulle in 1969. Not long before his departure from politics, the General had said that he looked forward to a France peopled by seventy million Frenchmen!

Perhaps, somewhat inadvertently, the reduced population did provide one advantage, France did not know anything like the level of unemployment that was the fate of Britain, America and Germany. Her figures ran into a few hundred thousands. Doubtless this was also due to technical reasons and to the fact of the existence of a large agricultural population, but the smaller population did help. It is only recently with the advent of the large postwar baby boom that France is now experiencing notable unemployment.

In the social welfare field the name of Pierre Laroque is pre-eminent. He had already proposed a Beveridge type of health and welfare system for France over a decade ago. Some of his proposals are only just now being realised. This is probably due to the fact that many of the needs have only recently arisen, but also due to the concern with other demands such as family allowances and military expenditure.

There is a much greater variety of philosophical schools in the strictly economic field. Interestingly enough, in this field one finds the economic philosopher, politicians, civil servants, bankers and business men very much mixed together. Nevertheless there are three distinct schools of thought – with naturally some compromise schools arising as the necessity demanded. In order of historical importance and application, one might call them the Classicists, the Planners and the Keynesians. The last school was a late-comer to France, the 'General Theory' only being translated into French in 1942, and Keynesian policies only being applied in the past two years.

At the strictly philosophical level, twentieth-century classical thinking and its application appears to have been strongly influenced by Labordère. This philosopher, who wrote two famous tracts in 1907[1] (and who incidentally seems to have had a strong influence on Robertson in the United Kingdom), supported the idea of the gold standard, stable currencies and strict banking policies. In view of the French experience with

[1] Marcel Labordère, '*Autour de la crise américaine de 1907 ou capitaux réels et capitaux apparents*', in *Revue de Paris* (1 February 1907).

inflation rather than with unemployment, it is not unexpected when we observe the influence of Labordère on the other side of the Channel. His main disciples, both in the interwar as well as during the postwar period, have been Rueff and Pinay, whose names have been associated with the famous plan of stabilisation and currency reform in 1958.[1]

M. Rueff, who is a member of the *Académie*, had great influence during the reign of General de Gaulle, and was largely responsible for advocating the realisation of the hard franc which was well on the way to becoming a reserve currency before the May events of 1968. Whether or not M. Rueff actually advocated the use of the franc as a reserve currency is not known. We do know however that in most of his writings and lectures he has always advocated the use of the gold standard in the international monetary field, and careful banking practices internally.[2]

Interestingly enough, although in the immediate postwar months, M. Mendès-France did not (and never did for that matter) advocate a return to the gold standard, he did advocate most careful and rather strict monetary management – similar to the policy adopted in Belgium and in Western Germany.

As one would have expected in the immediate postwar period, and indeed during the first four years of the Gaullist régime, the planners were paramount. Planning had been associated with the name of Jean Monnet, who pointed out that the State could influence more than 50% of the capital investment in the country – through its rôle as a financier, producer and employer. He emphasised the necessity of the State using this rôle, particularly during the immediate postwar years, in order to channel the scarce resources into the desired ends.

Subsequently the planning process was also used most effectively to remove bottlenecks in the economy. At all times the main aim was, however, the maintenance of a satisfactorily high level of capital investment in the country. During the first three plans, major budget deficits, foreign loans and aid, and devaluations were all used to help achieve this aim.

One of the other famous names associated with planning was

[1] This plan is discussed in some detail in Chapter 6.
[2] See, for example, M. Rueff, *Combat de l'ordre financier* (Plon, 1972).

that of Pierre Massé, one of the noted commissioners of the plan. He emphasised the rôle of the plan as an anti-chance element. By this he meant that with the use of its plan, France knew most of the time in which direction she was moving economically.

The gaullist politician who has strongly supported the views of both Monnet and Massé, is Michel Debré. Until Giscard d'Estaing took over the Finance Ministry in 1962, introducing his stabilisation Plan in the following year, Debré, the 'servant of the State', managed to enlist the support of the General for the Plan. Although the stabilisation plan was in part intended to re-introduce an element of Giscard d'Estaing's own economic liberalism into economic management, an attempt which is currently being repeated by the same individual, the businessmen did not appear to share the same outlook. Indeed, during the period 1962–5, private industrial investment actually fell.

Keynesian economics do occupy the final place in this section because, with the exception of a long practice of deficit budgets (mainly intended to maintain the level of capital investment), until 1970, the need never arose of consciously using Keynesian weapons in order to cut down the level of unemployment. But as soon as the necessity for using such weapons arose, they tended to be used with ingenuity and with flexibility.[1]

Interestingly enough, at the present time, under Giscard d'Estaing, all the philosophies described in this section are being used together. In the international monetary field, French official policy is strongly influenced by both Labordère and by Rueff. In the social field the reforms originally suggested over a decade ago by Laroque are finally being realised. The plan has been re-examined and appears to have found a second life. However, here, in order to make good the shortfall in savings, the private sector of the economy is being drawn in as a partner and the *Bourse* is being re-activated. Lastly, as already explained, a variety of Keynesian weapons are now being used with imagination and flexibility.

[1] These are described in some detail in Chapter 7.

2 External Affairs

No understanding of either France or Western Germany is possible without a serious examination of their external affairs. In both cases there has been one dominant problem in the postwar period; both countries have been intimately involved in the creation and evolution of the European Economic Community.

In the case of France, her very great problem had been that of the liquidation of her Empire, culminating in the bloody War of Algeria. It is to this subject that we should now turn.

France: The Colonies: Algeria

Already at the end of the 1920s, de Gaulle himself had understood the futility of the position of France in her colonies. This understanding had been gradually reinforced during the course of the Second World War. It is probable that had he been a completely free agent, and had he remained in power once the hostilities had ended, the French colonies might have gained a larger measure of independence. But this logical solution would not have been realised with ease largely because of the traditionally important rôle played by the army in France, by an army which had to efface the memory of the débâcle of 1939–40. The most obvious way of regaining the lost honour appeared to be through a victory in the colonial wars. When, in 1954, victory was no longer possible in Indo-China, the simultaneous opposition to a solution in North Africa, to Mendès-France and to a European Defence Force became ferocious. Indeed in 1954, due to the strong opposition of the French army leaders and of the right wing to any compromise in North Africa, and to the European Defence Force, there was a very grave risk of a military take-over in France. The subsequent veiled military take-over was simply postponed for four years, when paradoxically enough, de Gaulle, the only person the army would tolerate, was brought back to solve the Algerian crisis. Of course, most of his supporters in 1958 never dreamed for one moment that he was in fact to liquidate *L'Algérie Française* four years later.

Both the war in Algeria and the subsequent co-operation with that country had repercussions on France which are very difficult for the non-Frenchman to comprehend. Firstly the views of the army were not confined to the army and to the right-wing. Indeed, it was the grave vacillation of Guy Mollet, then Prime Minister of France, during his visit to Algeria (but particularly the City of Algiers) in 1956, which was the signal for the uprising among the settlers. Had M. Mollet simply remained in the colony for the full duration of his planned visit, it is certain that the movement among the settlers would have been much subdued. The reaction of Mollet was, to many left-wing supporters, simply a further betrayal of the left, which still further politicised the country into two principal political groups, the communists and the gaullists.

In the economic field, apart from the constant expenditure on defence since 1945, the Algerian situation had two profound economic consequences for France. One was the decision by the French State to force all petrol companies in France, whether French or foreign, to take most of their oil from the franc zone, which in effect, meant from Algeria. Secondly, the unexpected return of over a million settlers to metropolitan France in 1962 meant, on the one hand a political disequilibrium in the southern parts of the country, and on the other hand the sudden influx of a large mass of spending power into the economy – much spent on the speculative construction of luxury apartments – which entailed, in the following year, the effective dropping of the plan, and the introduction by Giscard d'Estaing of the stabilisation programme.

France: The European Economic Community

When de Gaulle returned to power in 1958, there were very grave doubts whether France would effectively become a member of the Common Market. These doubts were accentuated by the fact that the French Parliament had accepted the ratifying bill by the most slender of majorities, and by the fact that many French businessmen feared competition from their neighbours (particularly from Western Germany) once the tariff barriers were removed. It should be remembered that French industry had been relatively well protected by the tariff walls until she joined the Community. In reality, due to the high level of capital investment that had been undertaken since 1944, and to the two devaluations which took place in the course of the year of her accession to the European Economic Community, the French were far more competitive than they had originally imagined.

However when the General returned to power the situation was critically examined in some detail, and it was decided that France might gain more than she would lose from her membership. But, the campaign would be led on two fronts, political and economic. In the political field a means of extending the influence of France in Europe was seen.

It would be wrong to underestimate the desire by both de Gaulle (a desire previously held by M. Schuman) and of Adenauer to seek a rapprochement between the two countries. However the price asked for such a conversion was France's political dominance in the E.E.C. The use of French as the working language in the Commission Headquarters in Brussels was seen as an obvious asset. This was reinforced by the presence in Brussels of a top-class delegation of French civil servants (which included such personalities as M. Deniau). But, contrary to the desires of many federal Europeans of the 1940s and 1950s vintage (such as M. Monnet, for example), the gaullist view of Europe was, and still is, very much that of Europe of the nation states. In order to reinforce this view, the veto has been used, particularly with regard to Britain's earlier applications for membership of the Common Market. Of course many observers would maintain that the real reason for our rejection was Britain's close association with the United States.

This political view of France is quite easy to understand. Among the French authorities, particularly among the gaullists, there has always existed a certain suspicion about the links between Britain and the United States. This view was certainly vindicated by Britain's seeming inability to share their American atomic secrets with France and certainly by the statements made by many British politicians, both left- and right-wing, supporting Britain's 'special links' with America. More realistically, the fear has been more well-founded on the grounds of the enormous increase in the use of English throughout Europe and the swamping of France in the past decade by the anglo-saxon culture, particularly in the field of the theatre.

In the pure field of economics the rôle of France was quite
clear; she was not only to become the granary of Europe, but
also the main agricultural supplier of the Common Market.
Although she complained that industrial tariffs were removed
much more swiftly than agreement was reached on common

Table 1

FRENCH AGRICULTURAL EXPORTS TO HER NEIGHBOURS IN THE E.E.C.
1966–70
(As percentages of total agricultural trade)

	Exports			Imports		
	1966	*1968*	*1970*	*1966*	*1968*	*1970*
With E.E.C. countries	49	53	60	20	31	33
With franc zone	14	10	8	38	31	8
With other countries	37	37	32	42	38	32

agricultural prices, she nevertheless made enormous progress in
this field. Thus by 1966 France had already increased her
exports of agricultural goods to her five neighbours for which
the prices had already been fixed by over 500%! At the moment
of writing, the surplus trade position in agriculture of France
vis-à-vis her five partners can clearly be seen in Table 1. The
position is likely to improve now that Britain is a full member
of the Community.

A most important result of France's membership of the
Common Market was the enormous upsurge in foreign investment in the country. This upsurge came mainly from three

Table 2

NET FOREIGN INVESTMENT IN FRANCE
(In millions of dollars: rate of exchange as
in December 1964)

1955	+ 62·9	1960	+ 318·5
1956	+ 93·2	1961	+ 427·1
1957	+ 193·5	1962	+ 465
1958	+ 100·7	1963	+ 456·7
1959	+ 430·4	1964	+ 550·2

sources; from the United States, Switzerland and the United
Kingdom. These countries obviously wished to obtain a foothold

in the emerging Community, the latter two countries without necessarily becoming members themselves. The importance of these capital inflows is fairly obvious when one examines Table 2. However, of equal importance are the implications of Table 3, which show the key industries in which there is a heavy foreign interest.

Table 3

PERCENTAGE CONTROL IN KEY INDUSTRIES BY FOREIGN FIRMS 1963

Petrol: 60	Chemical industry: 25
(this was subsequently reduced due to the direct	
intervention of the French Government)	
Zinc: 80	Food production: 15
Mechanical industry: 25	Paper/Carton: 30
Electrical industry: 35+	

Table 3A

E.E.C.: PLACE IN FRENCH TRADE
(as a percentage of total)

	1959	1965	1968
Imports	28·0	38·8	47·3
Exports	29·0	40·9	42·9

3 Social Structure

This section of the book is crucially important regarding the study of France. If only to attempt an estimate of the future evolution of inflation in the country, we would have to examine the structure of the population. Then naturally linked with this important fact are the equally important considerations concerning the place of women in society, education and the trade unions.

The study of population has always occupied a leading place in the study of Economics in France. The name of one of France's leading economists, Alain Sauvy, has been almost exclusively associated with demographic studies. This concern with population is perfectly understandable. As was already mentioned in the first section, the country had lost the flower of its youth in the First World War. Subsequently, the outlawing of contraception in 1920, linked with the Napoleonic inheritance laws (whereby on the death of the father all the property had to be divided equally among all the children), tended to accentuate the critical heritage left by the war. Thus in 1939 15% of France's population was over the age of sixty. In other western countries, the percentage was as follows: the United Kingdom, 13·2; Germany, 12·4; Italy, 11·0; and the United States, 10·5. The problem in France was further heightened by the fact that more deaths were being recorded than births. The first constructive step to reverse this trend was the introduction of family allowances in 1932. These were further developed during the Vichy régime. At the end of the Second World War major increases were made, whilst in the single year of 1963 increases were made on three separate occasions! Thereafter the increases in these benefits tended not to keep pace with increases in the cost of living in the country. However the French family allowances are indeed varied and complex, and fundamentally generous. Basically an allowance is paid from the second child onwards. However where only one wage-earner exists in the family, payment is paid on the birth of the first child. Supplementary benefits (from the birth of the second child onwards) are paid when the child reaches the age of ten, and then again at the age of fifteen – it is considered that the needs of the child increase as it grows older. Normally the allowance finishes at the age of fifteen, but should the child continue professional

Table 4

THE POPULATION OF FRANCE
(In millions)

1900	1929	1938	1949	1968
39	41	42	41	50

training, the allowance continues until the age of eighteen (until the age of twenty where the child is in full-time education). Then for every child from the third one onwards, the basic allowance increases. The family allowances are financed by the employers on the basis of a tax which forms a percentage of the payroll.

Table 5

THE WORKING POPULATION OF FRANCE
(In thousands)

1949	1957	1965	1970
19,496	19,876	20,256	20,760

In view of the very generous level of family allowances in France, it would be reasonable to assume that the population would increase, and if we examine Table 4, we do note an important postwar increase in the French population; though we cannot assume this increase is solely due to the payment of family allowances.

This population growth in France has created its own problems. There is the basic imbalance in the population structure,

Table 6

THE POPULATION OF FRANCE
(Breakdown according to age in 1968)

	Percentage of total
Under 20	33·5
Between 20 and 64	54·0
Over 65	12·5

a small working population supports a large young and old population. Immigration has also produced its own problems. It has over the past decade been a somewhat haphazard affair,

Table 7

IMMIGRATION: FRANCE. FOREIGN WORKERS (EXCLUDING ALGERIANS*) TAKING UP PERMANENT RESIDENCE IN FRANCE
(Average per annum: in thousands)

1946–9	*1950–5*	*1956–8*	*1961–5*
50	18	85	120

(* There are currently over 500,000 Algerians resident in France.)

based on agreements with some countries (especially Algeria) rather than using selectivity as its criterion. This in turn has led to a large influx of relatively unskilled people who have not always been assimilated into the metropolitan population. Equally, cases of bad housing and other forms of prejudice against the immigrant population have not been uncommon.

A more immediately pressing problem at the present time, similar to the one being experienced in the United Kingdom, is that of the absorption of the large numbers of young workers coming on to the labour market. A major move (apart from the weapons described in the final part of this book) agreed upon between the main trade unions and the State in March 1972, was that of giving unemployment benefits to older workers amounting to 80% of their former salaries.

Apart from the reasons hitherto described, the situation has been aggravated further by the movement of population from the rural regions to the urban centres. Since there still exists a substantial part of the population engaged in agriculture, one cannot yet say that this movement has finished.

THE POSITION OF WOMEN IN FRENCH SOCIETY[1]

Many myths have been written about the position of women in French society. My own experience is that their position is strong! However we cannot allow ourselves to be swayed purely by subjective experiences. The best test of a woman's position in society would seem to be the degree of equality of pay that has been achieved between the sexes. In France the record is good.

A decree, dated 30 July 1946, removed hitherto accepted differences in basic wage rates, fixed by collective wage agreements between men and women. The preamble to the Constitution of 27 October 1946 (maintained in the Constitution of 4 October 1958), recognised the right of the equality of women with men in all fields, *des droits égaux à ceux de l'homme.*

In order to ensure equal minimum national wage rates for all workers, irrespective of age, sex and race, and intended especially to cover those workers not included in the collective wage agreements, a minimum national basic wage (S.M.I.G. *Salaire minimum interprofessionnel garanti*)[2] was introduced in 1949.

---

[1] Anglo-saxon readers are probably well aware of the eminent place that women have occupied in the literature of France down the ages. More recently, not only have Colette, Simone de Beauvoir, Françoise Sagan and Clara Malraux been concerned with the position of women in French society, but two writers (both prematurely dead), less well-known to readers outside France, have brought the attention of their compatriots to the position of women belonging to certain social categories, in modern French society. These two writers are Albertine Sarrazin (notably in *L'Astragal* and *La Cavale*, Pauvert, 1965) and, more recently, Gabrielle Russier, in *Lettres de Prison*, du Seuil, 1970.

[2] Re-named the S.M.I.C. – *Salaire minimum interprofessionnel de Croissance* on 2 January 1970. (The equivalent for agriculture is called the S.M.A.C.)

This measure has proved to be most important. It tends to be most rigidly applied and has been successful at times in raising the living standards of the lowest paid workers. Since the very important increases of 1968, it covers 12·5% of all employees, many of whom are women.

A law which came into effect on 11 February 1950 (*Labour Code*, book 1, article 31G) obliged collective agreements to accept the principle of 'equal work, equal pay' (*à travail égal, salaire égal*) for women and young people. The parties to collective agreements (since accepted by the courts) have interpreted this law as stipulating that 'for the same professional qualifications, women should receive the same pay as men'. In the professions, this does tend to be the accepted situation, and differs in most cases, substantially from the West German experience, and also somewhat from general British practice.

Apart from a basic lack of prejudice against female students (their numbers in the Universities are equal to those for male students) and against female workers, the economic evolution in France is particularly favourable to women.[1] Thus, for example, the number of women in the category 'unskilled labour' is declining twice as fast as the rate for men. Their numbers are, on the other hand, increasing in the executive classes, the professions, the service industries and in the growth sectors of the industrial economy.

Mention has already been made of the S.M.I.G. (now the S.M.I.C.). Until 1968 there existed different rates for the S.M.I.G., applicable to different regions. Surprisingly, for many Keynesians interested in regional development, the highest rate (similarly for family allowances) was in the Paris region, and not, as one might have expected, in Brittany. In June 1968, these *Taux d'abattement* disappeared, and at the same time the

---

[1] This evolution was particularly obvious during the period 1954–62. During this time the number of unskilled female workers increased by only 3%, whereas on the male side this was nearly 10%. In the service sector of the economy the increase among female employees was 28·5%, in the liberal professions and in the executive/management sections in commerce and in the civil service, the increase among women employees was 66%, whilst for men it was only 33%. Equally notable are the figures for the same period which show that the number of women employed in agriculture fell by 41·5%, and in textile/clothing by 13·6%. This should be compared with an increase of 42·1% in the electrical industry, 17·6% in the hotel trade and 40·9% in the civil service. One has the impression that women are taking over the management of the country!

S.M.I.G. was increased by 35% in the Paris region, and by 38% in the provinces.

Until this moment, the S.M.I.G. had applied to only 2% of the workers; after June 1968, it covered 12·5% of the work force. The biggest increases in wages (to bring the basic wage into line with the S.M.I.G.) were in the textile and clothing industries – which tended to employ many women. Consequently, the difference between men's and women's wages, which stood at 9·5% in April 1968, fell to 7·3% in July of the same year.

In the State enterprises, in the public administration (the civil service and teaching), in the liberal professions and in the upper reaches of industry, there exists complete equality of pay for men and women in the same job categories. Similarly, in France, women are more likely to be placed in the job category which corresponds to their qualifications.

EDUCATION

Since the May Events of 1968, French education has been the centre of tumultuous upheaval. The upheavals themselves tended to mask a fundamental problem in French University education, that of the ever-increasing masses of students entering the Universities – with a system of selection operating in only a few faculties. The famous Faure Reforms did not solve this grave problem, but rather tended to confirm the Grandes Ecoles in their supremacy. Perhaps this was to be expected in a country which boasts a Normalien as its President! However, before examining the French University system, and in particular the Faure Reforms, it is both useful and necessary to examine the pre-University education as it exists in France.

(i) *The Nursery Schools: 'Les Maternelles'*

If French education wishes to select any part of its system for particular praise, that honour would most certainly be given to the nursery schools, the famous *Ecoles Maternelles*. In their human and progressive attitude to their charges, they may easily be compared with the very best English infant schools.

Normally, French children may attend these schools from

the age of three onwards. In special cases, and where places are available, children may be admitted before the age of three. These schools become more and more popular. In the Paris region, where the demand for places is high, there is a grave insufficiency of such schools and the requisite teaching staff. This has led to the existence of long waiting lists for any places which may become available.

(ii) *Primary School: Secondary School*

At the age of seven, French children enter the primary school, which they normally attend for a period of five years, entering the secondary school at about the age of twelve.

Only two innovations of note have been made in the primary schools. One is the introduction of modern mathematics, which has caused a major furore among French teachers and academics in general. Perhaps, fortunately, the French Government has come down heavily in its support of the continuance of this experiment – largely on the grounds that this will remove the possibility of the production of a mathematical élite, controlling the mass of the population.

The other change has been the dropping of the examination which pupils normally had to pass before entering class six.[1]

Before examining the secondary schools in any depth, it should be noted that French education is compulsory until the age of sixteen. Although education in secondary schools is very broad (comprising some fifteen subjects, which are taught right the way through from class six until the end, with normally some specialisation from class two onwards – in special situations from class five), some means have had to be found of catering for those who wish to leave school after the age of sixteen or simply for weak pupils. These have taken the form of the organisation of 'transitional classes' in the Lycées or the C.E.S. (*Collèges d'Enseignement Secondaire*), which provide either a form of vocational training, or supplementary help for somewhat backward pupils who wish to rejoin the mainstream of secondary education at a later date.

In French secondary schools, there are two distinct 'cycles'. The first cycle, which caters for all pupils, is given in the

---

[1] Contrary to British practice, French class numbers start at the large end of the scale and finish at number one.

municipal C.E.S. These cater for pupils from the sixth to the third classes, inclusive.

The second cycle is created for those pupils who wish to continue their studies after the age of sixteen. Here, pupils have the choice of three types of institutes. These are the rather more traditional State Lycée,[1] the more modern, somewhat vocational State Lycée Technique, and the strictly practical and vocational C.E.T. (*Centres d'Enseignement Technique*). The latter institutes are not particularly highly esteemed by the more traditional academics.

At this point it is worth examining the different certificates and qualifications which are obtainable from the different institutes. But first one should note that the famous *Certificat d'Etudes Primaires* is gradually disappearing from the educational scene.

Normally a fairly general certificate is offered to pupils in the third class. This is the *Brevet d'Enseignement de Premier Cycle*. This qualification seems to be a form of compromise, being superior to the old *Certificat d'Etudes Primaires* and inferior to the first *Baccalauréat* which was abolished in 1965. This former first *Baccalauréat* has been merged with the second one which is obtained at the end of one's secondary studies. Although, in Britain, we try to compare the *Baccalauréat* with our Advanced Level General Certificate, we should note that a much broader level of culture is demanded in France than is the case in the United Kingdom. Despite the steady move towards specialisation in France, the situation still bears no comparison with the rather premature and frequently disastrous specialisation which we experience in Britain.

This move towards specialisation in France begins in the second class.[2] The *Baccalauréat* A and B are literary-orientated (A covering the classics, B modern languages). The C and D categories are scientific, whilst the categories E and T cover economics and technical subjects.

[1] The Lycée corresponds somewhat to the British grammar school.
[2] Since 1969 however an examination in French has been re-introduced. It is taken in the first class and counts as part of the *Baccalauréat* taken the following year.

THE UNIVERSITIES: THE FAURE PLAN[1]

As we have already noted, the Faure Plan has not really solved the fundamental problem of French University education – the masses of students entering the Universities. The lack of selection and the consequent inevitable lack of contact between staff and students (due to the huge numbers of students) mean that between 70 and 75% of French University students never receive a degree. Economically and socially, the situation is not improved by the fact that normally not more than 30% of French students receive a grant which can be equivalent to between *1400 francs* and *4200 francs* per annum. Consequently, the number of students from working-class backgrounds rarely exceeds 12% of the total student population.

The Faure Reforms also did not affect (rather they confirmed the superiority of these institutions) the *Grandes Ecoles*. This is a serious matter for the Universities. We should not forget that the *Grandes Ecoles* do cream off a certain elite of the French youth. They are strictly competitive, entry being gained after being accepted among the top few in an examination which is taken after two years of the most intensive (and rather in-human) preparation in a few specialised Lycées in Paris. Frequently, when the members of the *Grandes Ecoles* have obtained their first degree, they will compete for the *Agrégation*. If they obtain this qualification, they are quite untouchable. Although a test of this unquestionable excellence exists nowhere in the anglo-saxon world – and it has produced some excellent people – it must be questioned whether the creaming-off of a small élite in this competitive manner is really the best thing for a modern state and its Universities.

Thus the Faure Reforms were concerned with the old faculties and their attendant institutes and the excellent *Instituts Universitaires de Technologie*, all of which were formerly strictly controlled from Paris. In fact, the understandable demands for university autonomy (and its subsequent granting) tended to

[1] In November 1973, a further change will take place, when the D.E.U.G. (Diplôme d'Etudes Universitaires Générales) will be introduced. This will be awarded after the successful completion of two years of University studies. The licence would then be awarded at the end of the third year, the Maîtrise at the end of the fourth.

obscure the fundamental problems which we have already examined.

The reforms then were based on the two criteria of autonomy and participation. In name, the groupings of old faculties and sections became the new *Unités d'Enseignement et de Recherche*, the U.E.R.s. The creation of these groupings seems however to have been physically based on the criteria of numbers of students on the one hand, and on the similarity of disciplines on the other. For teaching and research purposes, the old faculties and sections remain. The desired inter-disciplinary participation takes place in the councils of the Universities.

It is questionable whether the French will accept a system of selection which we know in Britain. Whilst tolerating the existence of the *Grandes Ecoles*, the suggestion that centres for the training of all teachers should be set up – but to which entry and qualifications should be by competition, based on a pre-arranged set annual number of diplomas – has, in 1972, set off a series of demonstrations and strikes in most French Universities.

If the Faure Reforms have achieved anything, they have organised the allocation of greater resources to the Universities. It should be noted that for the first time substantial resources have been devoted to sporting and social ends. Also, whilst

Table 8

NUMBER OF UNIVERSITY STUDENTS

		1967–8	1968–9
	Total Students	Female Students	Total Students
	509,898	221,447	575,366
Division by Discipline			
Law	102,721	31,423	126,696
(and associate disciplines)			
Sciences	110,258	37,159	123,347
Arts	165,190	109,100	196,144
Medicine	82,423	24,644	98,428
Pharmacy	17,735	10,347	20,517
Multi-discipline centres	—	—	10,234

the new found administrative autonomy may have created problems, not least of all financial, the institutes no longer have to ask the permission of Paris if they wish to purchase the smallest article – as was formerly the case. In an equally important field, the Universities (permissible since 1972) may now make important exchanges with foreign Universities. However, as before, the respectability of degrees and diplomas is decided nationally, in Paris.

The newly-created participation has been the fruit of heated controversy since some observers believe that few people participate, whilst others believe that the new liberty is an occasion for political confrontation between different groups, particularly between the communists and gaullists. Whatever the real political situation may be in each establishment, the fact remains that the University Council (the governing body) is elected by staff, students and personnel, and that this Council then elects the Vice-Chancellor or Director of the Institute. Thus, the system appears to be highly democratic.

TRADE UNIONS

The Constitution of France guarantees the right to form trade unions. This fundamental right has been somewhat questioned since the passing of the law in 1963, making compulsory a notice of five days (a *Préavis*) by unions in the public sector and nationalised industries who plan to go on strike. The difficulties of the unions are not eased by the fact that workers who go on strike do not receive any form of subsistence from public funds.

Until the events of 1968, when the communist-led trade unions did not take over the country – as most observers had believed they would – French trade unions had been regarded as political pressure groups. Indeed (as will be seen from the descriptive part at the end of this section), except where the unions are obvious professional pressure groups, for example, the union for executives, they tend to have quite obvious political colours which make their counterparts in other western nations look rather pale at their side. However, even a few years before 1968, the changing rôle of the unions was becoming obvious, they were becoming economic pressure groups. This was becoming particularly clear in two related fields. Firstly, in order to support wage claims, there might be a series of lightning, revolving or prolonged sympathy strikes in different public or nationalised sectors of the economy. This was particularly the case in 1963 when strikes took place in the coal, railway, electricity and metal sectors of the economy. In the case of the miners, the strikes were prolonged and included a march on Paris by the miners and the occupation of the mines by the State by way of retaliation.

Secondly, the unions do have a legal right to participation in company and national economic affairs. They are officially represented (though their numbers are still too small here) on the Planning Commission and participate in the elaboration of the National Plan. They are also represented on the *Conseil Economique et Social* and on all upper councils in all ministries relating to economic and social affairs. In the case of individual companies with more than ten employees, delegates of the personnel must be accepted and a company committee (*Comité d'Entreprise*) must be set up. In the latter case, such committees only exist in firms with more than fifty employees. These committees can be consulted on all economic and social problems relating to the firm. This vague ruling gave much freedom of interpretation to employers and it is only through the gaullist obsession with participation (as manifested notably in the *Amendement Vallon*) that the influence of unions has become a reality. This has been shown by the agreement between the major unions and the Ministry of Labour in 1971 to introduce wage payments on a monthly salaried basis, and the agreement made in March 1972 between the Ministries of Finance and Labour and the main unions to enable older unemployed workers to receive up to 80% of their normal wages in the form of unemployment benefits.

Previous to the major moves towards participation, the unions had always exerted an important influence in obtaining pathbreaking social and material benefits in the nationalised industries and in the public sector. The tendency was for the achievements made in these sectors to be emulated in subsequent years by the private sectors of the economy. The most important precursor in the nationalised industrial sector has been the Renault car firm. Already at the end of 1963, a fourth week of paid holidays was obtained by workers in this firm. In subsequent years, this extra week has tended to be granted to firms in the private as well as in the public sector of the French economy.

Trade Unions: Glossary

C.G.T.: *Confédération Générale du Travail*
The communist trade union which is very important and the largest union. It probably has nearly two million members. The president is Georges Séguy.

C.G.T. – *F.O.*: *Force Ouvrière*
The non-communist, but socialist union, formed in 1947 after the rupture with the C.G.T. In 1966 it had 600,000 members. Most of its members are drawn from civil servants and workers in nationalised industries.

C.F.D.T.: *Confédération Française Démocratique du Travail*
This was originally a union with strong Roman Catholic leanings. Now it is a secular movement with a Christian Democrat political colour.

C.F.T.C.: *Confédération Française des Travailleurs Chrétiens*
This is the splinter group of about 80,000 members which broke away when the main movement became the C.F.D.T.

F.E.N.: *Fédération de l'Education Nationale*
The trade union for teachers – it has about 400,000 members.

C.G.C.: *Confédération Générale des Cadres*
The trade union for executives. It has naturally only a small number of members, 200,000 in all.

S.N.E.S.: *Syndicat National de l'Enseignement Supérieur*
This organisation would correspond to the British Association of University Teachers.

At this point we should note that since at any one time only between 20% and 25% of the workers in France belong to a trade union, the effectiveness of trade union activity must at all times be somewhat limited. It is obviously most effective when one or more public services are completely affected.

C.G.P.M.E.: *Confédération Générale des Petites et Moyennes Entreprises*

During both the 1950s, the 1960s, and even at the present time, this association of shopkeepers and the owners of small and medium-sized businesses has caused the authorities some discomfort through their demonstrations. The activity of this association has tended to increase as the livelihood of its members has been increasingly threatened by the expansion of super- and hyper-markets and the imposition of heavy taxes. The French State is about to introduce a tax on the super- and hyper-markets which will apparently be used to subsidise the small shops. One of the most famous leaders of the C.G.P.M.E. has been Gérard Nicoud, who has been imprisoned for his actions.

C.N.P.F.: *Congrès National du Patronat Français*

The French equivalent of the British C.B.I.

C.G.A.: *Confédération Générale de l'Agriculture*

It was the Vichy Government which imposed a corporate organisation on French agriculture. Later under a Socialist Minister (Tanguy-Prigent) the C.G.A. was formed. Inevitably, distrust and friction arose between the rich farmers of Central France who owned large areas of land and the smaller and poorer farmers in the south and elsewhere. This friction led to the formation of the:

F.N.S.E.A.: *Fédération Nationale des Syndicats d'Exploitants Agricoles*

In turn this inevitable friction within the farming community was accentuated still further by the generation gap which led to the formation of yet another group, the

C.N.J.A.: *Centre National des Jeunes Agriculteurs.*

MEDICAL CARE IN FRANCE

This area of social economics has always been most controversial. The medical profession in France, as in most other western countries, has always jealously guarded its monopolistic position. It has ensured that the numbers entering the profession have never upset this monopoly. In view of the long and costly studies (and one must remember that only a minority of French students receive scholarships – in themselves normally materially insufficient to maintain a decent standard of living) and the exorbitant costs of setting up a medical practice, it is no wonder that the monopoly has remained and that the salaries of both doctors and chemists alike have remained high. Also, the sons of members of the medical profession have tended to enter that profession. Of late there have been considerable upheavals in the medical faculties and students have demanded the adoption of the equivalent of the British national health service. This does not mean that France has had no health service, rather that doctors were not compelled to belong to it and that reimbursement to patients for treatment has rarely been complete. In fact, with the exception of persons who are really too poor to pay, the maximum reimbursement is 80% of the costs of treatment.

The agreement to which the doctors adhere is the *Convention de la Sécurité Sociale*. Hitherto, the main objection which doctors held against this system was that the fees allowed under this agreement were not as high as some members of the profession desired. This meant that until quite recently, only 39% of the doctors in Lyon, 64% in Grenoble and 50% in Paris were members of the Convention. This fact naturally restricted the choice of poorer patients to a limited number of doctors.

In October 1971, a new Convention was signed and led to a 96% membership of the system. The new agreement was more flexible than the previous ones. Firstly the agreement will be renewed every two years. In contrast with past contracts, which were by no means uniform, the new Convention allows doctors to withdraw as individuals should they so desire. Also the C.S.M.F. (*Confédération des Syndicats Médicaux Français*) is responsible for the good behaviour of its members *vis-à-vis* the *Sécurité Sociale*, and may remove any members from the agreement should their conduct warrant such action.

The real reason for this volte-face by French doctors has been the important exceptions or dérogations which have been built into the new system. Thus doctors may now charge a patient a fee for treatment in excess of that laid down in the Convention. The patient however will be reimbursed only at the rates laid down in the agreement and has thus to make up the difference himself or herself.

The salaries earned by both doctors and chemists in France have been notoriously high. In a study published by the C.R.E.D.O.C.,[1] the average salary earned by doctors in 1969 who actually belonged to the Convention was 97,700 francs! It is therefore not surprising that the percentage of the gross national product devoted to medical care in France appears to be high when compared with other countries.

The account of the recent 'accords' signed in France between the French Medical Association and the *Sécurité Sociale* should not lead readers to assume that all problems in this field have been solved and that the philosophical ferment has ceased. In the latter case, a host of thinkers, writers and critics have joined Pierre Laroque, the French equivalent of Beveridge, and they bitterly criticise the class consciousness of French medical studies and treatment.[2] They also criticise the inadequate resources devoted to medicine in France and, as elsewhere in Europe, they propose that greater emphasis be placed both on preventive treatment and on more specialised medicine.

As in other countries, there is considerable concern at the decreasing number of nurses in French hospitals. A study, conducted in 1968, showed that each year 10% of the lay nurses in French hospitals definitely leave the profession.[3] The seriousness of this situation is heightened by the fact that the nurses who leave the profession are not being replaced at the same rate. This lack of replacement means that some hospitals and clinics are being closed through lack of personnel.[4]

A final point of concern among most of the writers cited in this section is that until 1967 the control of the organisations to which the finances of the social security services were entrusted, the *Caisses de la Sécurité Sociale*, were heavily weighted in favour of the employees as represented by their trade unions. In 1967 the control of these organisations passed into the

[1] *Centre de Recherches et de Documentation sur la Consommation.*
Mathé, *La Santé est-elle au-dessus de nos moyens?* (Plon, 1970). G. Caro, *La*
[2] See: J. C. Polack, *La Médecine du capital* (F. Maspero, 1971). C. and G. *Médecine en question* (Maspero, 1967). M. Bosquet, 'La Réforme de la Sécurité sociale' (*Nouvelle Observateur*, 27 July 1970). B. C. Savy, *Nouvelle Politique de santé* (Editions Universitaires, 1969).
[3] J. Baudot and C. Vilmont, 'Enquiry into Nursing in Public Hospitals' in the journal, *Population* No. 3 (1968).
[4] Dr. L. Marion, 'La France manque d'infirmières' (*Le Monde*, 4 November 1970).

control of the employers. It is perhaps somewhat surprising that nothing was done to change this situation in 1968; perhaps it represents a changing shift of interest among French trade unions.

CONCLUSIONS

It is difficult to draw any definite conclusions in a field as wide as the social structure of a country such as France. We do know that despite the relatively small working population in France – which has to support a large number of young and old people (and which leads to some degree of sectoral inflation) – we nevertheless have an unusually high degree of unemployment among young people in the country which can be taken as yet another indicator of structural imbalance in the economy.

We know that the trade unions are not terribly strong but that important industrial wage agreements favourable to the Unions have been made, especially in such nationalised concerns as *Electricité de France* and *Renault*. In the latter case, an agreement has just been made which fixes the minimum monthly wage at 1500 francs.[1] Since such concerns are normally regarded as national pace-setters, the implications of this agreement are obvious.

However it is necessary to make some qualitative conclusion at this point, and the conclusion which would be necessary should refer to the degree of social mobility in France. In examining the educational and the medical systems, doubts have been expressed about the degree of social mobility in the country. In March 1966, the I.N.S.E.E. published a study in its journal *Etudes et Conjoncture*, concerning the social mobility in France. This study confirmed the fairly rigid state of social mobility in the country. The general picture was one of a country in which the son would normally follow in his father's footsteps professionally – at least at the start of his working life.

Examining the situation in France since 1959, the study concluded that 41·6% of the sons of farmers were employed in agriculture, and among industrial workers, 74·4% of the sons were in the same activity as their fathers. Possibly of

[1] June 1972.

greater importance is the conclusion that the social milieu quite considerably influences the type of education a child is likely to receive. It is quite common for the children of parents with comfortable incomes to undertake long studies – among modest income groups such a phenomenon is indeed rare. Among professional groups 55% of children pursue higher studies; among agricultural workers' children only 0·1 % go on to higher education. Thus a situation develops where children, through the type of education to which they have access, are most likely to remain in the social group in which they are born.

4 Industry and Agriculture

Originally the author planned to give the following title to this chapter: Ownership of Industry. Since however this chapter is concerned primarily with the structure (which must of course include ownership) of industry and agriculture, and with the distributive system in France, the word 'ownership, was dropped from the title. There will certainly be some criticism of this decision since many observers will consider that the problems of these two sectors of the French economy are partly due to the large number of individual owners in the country. In this section, nevertheless, it is hoped that this observation will to some degree be refuted. Certainly in the field of distribution we shall see that there has been something of a revolution in France during recent years, and that the tale of all farm produce being transported first to Les Halles in Paris and then out again to the provinces is now little more than a myth.

INDUSTRY

Industry, like agriculture, has been plagued by a multitude of small units of production. Even in 1969, 75% of the total national industrial turnover was accounted for by only 11% of all the industrial enterprises in the country, whilst the top seven hundred enterprises accounted for three-quarters of France's exports. Excluding individual artisans, there were in 1968 175,000 small and medium sized business enterprises. M. de Lannurien[1] maintains that in 1966, at least a third of all businesses did not declare any profits at all! This would seem to indicate that the leading firms must be very good indeed. Further, the record of industrial productivity in France has been most satisfactory since the last war. Most observers would agree that one of the main reasons for this fact has been the satisfactorily high level of capital investment that has been maintained

[1] P. de Lannurien, *Cent ans de retard.*

throughout most of this period, thus placing mainly new equipment at the disposal of French workers.

However, as in agriculture, the State has wished to encourage the merging of enterprises together in order to enable France to compete more effectively within the Common Market. Spontaneous take-overs in the country, such as the attempt by the energetic company Boussois, to take over the less-energetic St. Gobain in 1969, tend to be rare. Rather the State actively encourages mergers. Thus, although the law of 1951 enabled firms in shipbuilding to merge (with governmental financial support), it was only in 1960–1, after threats by the government, that the first mergers were made.[1] Correspondingly the French Government is anxious not to allow take-overs of French businesses by foreign firms when it considers that such an act would be contrary to the national interest. Thus considerable negotiations took place before General Electric were allowed to take over Machines Bull in 1964; and the approval of the government had to be obtained before the agreements could be signed between Fiat and Citroën in 1968. As will be shown in the section devoted to energy, France is certainly not opposed to monopoly, especially where this happens to be controlled by the State or where there is an active State participation; but she is more concerned about foreign domination of key sectors of her economy. The recent creation of the I.D.I. (*Institut de Développement Industriel*) might be seen as an attempt to reinforce the competitive strength of French firms in the European Economic Community.

The self-financing of French firms has been relatively weak (see Table 28) when compared with Britain and Western Germany. This fact, linked with the rather conservative attitude of the banks, led to basic reforms of the banking structure in 1966 (see Chapter 6) and the current reforms being introduced in the *Bourse* in France. It is hoped that these reforms will complement current financing of industry from traditional sources.

France has problem industries similar to those of Britain – coal, shipbuilding and to a certain degree, the iron and steel industry. Mention has already been made of attempts (wrongly

[1] The following mergers were noted for the listed years: 1957, 450; 1961, 2,000; and 1965, 1600.

the author would maintain) to help the shipbuilding industries through the giving of grants and enforced mergers. Some help is also being given to the mines, yet consumption of coal is constantly falling and the movement of population from the mining areas continues. In the case of iron and steel, the major aid for the workers in Lorraine is through the possibility of receiving help for their transfer to the huge steel plant currently being built at Fos in Southern France. This form of assistance should really be placed in the category of regional policy and aid which is examined in Chapter 5, in the first section. In its magnitude however the Fos operation does surpass any industrial and regional development ever undertaken in France with State help and probably it will become a prototype for future ventures.

The financing and control of French industry has often, outside France, been seen solely in the framework of the Plan.[1] Certainly, as is indicated in Chapter 6, the strict control of credit in the immediate postwar years ensured that industry normally complied with the wishes of the government as expressed in the National Plan.[2] With the passage of time, the upsurge of foreign investment in France – partly as a result of her membership of the European Economic Community – and the desire of de Gaulle to associate the workers more closely with both managerial and financial participation in industry, the financing and control of French industry have changed. As is indicated in Table 28, the decline in the self-financing of French firms may accelerate this process.

To date,[3] and including the notable distribution of shares in the nationalised Renault automobile company, 6800 agreements have been signed, covering 7577 enterprises and 3,500,000 workers.

It is perhaps an unfortunate defect of the Anglo-Saxons that they tend to equate size with efficiency and profitability. In examining French firms, we have already noted that a minority of strong firms are responsible for a high percentage of both internal turnover and exports. Apart from the sudden recent

---

[1] Probably the best account of the French planning apparatus and the execution of the successive plans is given in B. Cazes, *La Planification en France et le IVe Plan* (Les Editions de L'Epargne, 1962).

[2] A good account of this control is given in M. Lagache, *La Politique du Crédit* (Les Editions de L'Epargne, 1963).

[3] April 1971, based on the law of 1968.

explosion in the number and size of the *Hypermarchés* (which M. Lepage of *L'Entreprise* now believes to be past its peak), the statistics do indicate that the number of business enterprises in France which employ either small or medium numbers of employees has remained surprisingly stable over the past fifteen years. (See Table 9 below.) However, as the following figures would indicate, on a European basis, the profitability of some of the leading French firms is admirable. In some cases this may be due to the policy of the French State in encouraging

Table 9

INDUSTRIAL CONCENTRATION:
DIVISION OF INDUSTRIAL WORKING
POPULATION BY ENTERPRISE
(As percentage of total number of enterprises)

Number of employees per enterprise	1954	1962	1966
0	6·0	5·0	4·0
1–4	13·0	11·0	10·0
5–9	6·0	5·0	6·0
10+	75·0	79·0	80·0

NUMBER OF ENTERPRISES (1955 = 100) IN 1966

General	
Mechanical industries	91
Automobile/Cycle	50
Electro-mechanic	97
Chemical engineering	90
Textiles	74
Clothing	71
Wood and Furnishing	83

some monopolies or oligopolies as being 'healthy' and in discouraging others as being 'unhealthy'.[1] To this we must emphasize the importance of the consistently satisfactory level of capital investment in the country, the high salaries paid to chief executives, export managers and engineers (who undergo a much longer training and 'education' than is the case in Britain)

[1] This is, in fact, the responsibility of the *Commission Technique des Ententes et des Positions Dominantes*, examined in more detail on page 33.

and the general rigorous business climate which has increasingly pervaded France since her entry into the European Economic Community.

It is noticeable that shortly after de Gaulle's return to power, and following the publication of the national economic reforms suggested by M. Rueff and M. Pinay, a report had also been prepared by M. Armand and M. Rueff, suggesting that a number of short- and long-term reforms be introduced by French business.[1] However the only suggestion really heeded by M. Debré

Table 10

AGE OF MACHINE TOOLS USED IN INDUSTRY

	Less than 5 years	5–10 years	10–20 years	20–30 years	30+ years
	(As percentage of total)				
1955	20·2	22·4	15·8	15·7	25·9
1960	24·0	18·0	19·8	18·9	19·3
Degree of depreciation	8·0 %	25·0 %	50·0 %	83·0 %	100·0 %

Source: Carré, Dubois et Malinvaud, *La Croissance française*, p. 181 (du Seuil, 1972).

was that concerning the encouragement to increase in private house construction and that rents be freed from control (except in certain special cases of course, and not including the H.L.M.).

The real critique of French business alone came from the former Treasurer of the war-time *Résistance* and the present President of the *Crédit Lyonnais*, M. Bloch-Laîné.[2]

M. Bloch-Laîné was concerned with the lack of participation by shareholders in French industry and business (the Company Law in this respect had remained unchanged since 1867, and was only to be reformed in July 1966) and by the lack of worker participation in industry and in business (here he was already anticipating the *Amendement Vallon*).

The *Rapport Rueff-Armand* (1960) is worth examining in somewhat greater detail. The Report made the following very important suggestions:

(i) That expansion was the necessary environment in which the economy could transform itself.

[1] *Rapport sur les obstacles à l'expansion économique* (Paris, 1960).
[2] F. Bloch-Laîné, *Pour une réforme de l'entreprise* (du Seuil, 1963).

(ii) That the sheer proliferation of rules and regulations regarding France's economic management could only reinforce the rigidity of the existing system.

(iii) Both the professional uniformity and the homogeneity of the working week in France were criticised.

(iv) The great French tradition of a homogeneous work timetable each day for the whole population, and the fact that the bulk of the French population takes its summer holiday in August, could only impair the correct use of the country's infrastructure.

(v) The Report was particularly critical of continuing the provision of subsidies for non-productive industries. Here the steel industry, and in particular the Forges d'Hennebont (which should have long since been closed down) were the objects of bitter criticism.

(vi) The psychological influence of 'traditionalism' was also heavily criticised.

(vii) The Report noted that the very structure of the administrative system (its divisions) impeded the government from taking the changes which might be necessary in France.

(viii) The Report found that the narrow outlook of institutions and of people in France impeded progress.

(ix) A plea (only finally heeded in the Sixth and current national Plan) for a more equal division of the national wealth was made.

(x) Finally, the out of date educational system was accused of maintaining an equally out of date *status quo* in French society.

Monopoly Control and the Restructuring of French Industry

The *Commission Technique des Ententes et Positions Dominantes* was created in 1953. The rôle given to this body was to examine mergers and firms with dominant market positions whose activities may be against the law.[1]

The influence of this *Commission* appears to have been greatest in the field of mergers. There are simply some mergers which are regarded as being 'good' and some as being 'bad'.

---

[1] This meant that the business practices did not lead to an improvement in productivity, rather the aim was to prevent, restrict or upset market competition.

Certainly, 'good' mergers will improve France's international competitive position, 'bad' ones would harm the internal national market.

In the field of restrictive practices, the number of cases coming before the Commission has always been limited. During the period 1955–9, only twenty cases were examined. During the period 1960–8, an average of six cases a year were examined.

At first little or no publicity was given to the deliberations of the Commission. There were also no legal proceedings taken against firms which had infringed the law. Instead it was felt that a ministerial directive was an adequate weapon. Since 1959 the decisions of the Commission have been published in the *Journal Officiel*, and since 1966, in certain cases legal proceedings have been taken against some firms.

Once again, it is important to remember that it has long been a French tradition to favour and indeed to actively encourage monopolies whenever these have been considered to have been in the national interest. The monopolies, through the very force of both economic and political factors, may take different forms, e.g. the monopolistic position of the *Compagnie Française des Pétroles*, the special position of the O.R.T.F., or the steady erosion of the independent French regional press through take-overs by major newspaper concentrations. In 1972, there was the important example of the clash between the majority of the employees of *Paris-Normandie* and a major national newspaper chain which desired to take over this regional newspaper based on Rouen. The disappearance of the excellent regional press in France could only lead to a reduction in the quality of life, at a time when there appears to be a serious desire to revive the strength of the major regional centres.

Indeed one is led to question this obsession with size. A number of medium-sized French firms frequently producing quality articles, would appear to be highly competitive at the international level. In some traditional spheres such as food, wine, perfumes, fashion and luxury articles, some centres such as London and Rome may experience short-lived flashes of greatness, but the French dominance in these fields remains unchallenged. In other fields too, at an international level, as Table 16 at the end of this section indicates, France is competitive.

The setting up of the I.D.I. in 1970 marked a departure in

French economic and industrial policy. This organisation, which has important public funds at its disposal (200 million francs in 1970, 400 in 1971 and 400 in 1972), has been given the largest possible freedom of action and will not be forced to help firms of questionable viability which the government itself might wish, for other reasons, to support. Basically the aim of this organisation is to help medium-sized and nationally potentially important firms to enable them to expand without difficulty. In 1972 the I.D.I. took a participation in eight firms or industrial groups at a cost of 360 million francs. These participations ranged from the firm *Logabax*, which makes small computers, to the *Briqueteries Rivière et Letort*, in Brittany. In the former case, the aid was necessary as the company had to make heavy investments in the face of an anticipated increase in demand of 25%. In the second case, the aim (in conjunction with the *Société de Développement Régional de la Bretagne*) is to help to diversify the product mix of the brickworks through the production of light-weight building elements for which the demand is increasing.

When examining the choice of ventures chosen for participation by the I.D.I., one notes two elements common to all the ventures. They are in all cases, firms or groups producing modern products for which the demand is increasing. They are also frequently situated in regions which might normally qualify for some form of regional aid. The I.D.I. seems therefore to combine a policy of industrial and regional help – but of a dynamic nature.

Energy

France's record in this field has been good. One of the indirect results of her successful energy policy has been the successful completion of the twenty-year plan for the modernisation and electrification of the French railways, on time, in December 1965.

As the following table indicates, the trend in France, as in Britain, has been away from the use of coal to the use of oil. There has been a gradual closing-down of inefficient coal-mines and an increase in oil imports. Likewise, there has been, heavily financed by the State and public share issues, a substantial, though by no means comparable increase in the production of hydro-electric power. Whilst France has made little headway in the production of nuclear energy, she has been at the top of the European league table in the field of the harnessing of both solar and tidal energy.

It is in the field of energy where the '*dirigiste*' policy of the French State is best seen in practice in industrial and business affairs. In particular, the policy regarding oil and petroleum deserves our attention. A law promulgated in 1928 gave the

Table 11

ENERGY: CONSUMPTION
(Equivalent to millions of tons of coal)

	1938	1949	1957	1960	1965	1970	1975 (*est.*)
Coal, coke	67·5	71·6	79·8	70·2	70·0	63·65	57·0
Petroleum, oil	9·2	13·8	28·1	39·0	74·0	94–100	124–136
Hydro-electricity	7·2	6·6	14·9	16·1	17·1	20·0	23·0
Gas	—	0·3	0·7	4·5	9·0	15·0	23·0
Nuclear energy	—	—	—	—	0·4	3·6	10·0
Total	83·9	92·3	123·5	129·8	170·0	198–202	237–249

State great powers concerning the importation and refining of oil. This law has been used to make France as independent as possible in the provision and distribution of this form of energy. Following success in obtaining oil-prospecting holdings in countries belonging to the franc zone, the government made special contracts with companies in 1959 and 1963, by which they agreed to refine certain surplus quantities of oil from the franc zone (mainly from the Sahara). At the same time, the State used its powers to force certain foreign petroleum companies to sell out to French companies. It went so far (in a decree dated 28 February 1963) as to determine how far the French market should be divided. By 1965, French companies controlled half of the home market.

The Service and Distributive Industries

Until very recently, it was relatively uncommon for foreign observers to consider France as being part of the 'affluent society', and yet, already by 1964, her consumption of consumer durables was equal to that of Western Germany. As a member of the *Société des Gadgets*, France becomes more and more like the United States of America. There is a frantic obsession with cars and household gadgets and the population becomes more and more mesmerised by the television programmes (themselves frequently of doubtful quality) and until very recently the population was consuming more and more pharmaceutical products. Spending on services of all kinds has been increasing (as the following tables indicate) much more greatly than spending on food and on clothing. Likewise the numbers of persons employed in the service sectors has increased to such a degree that this is now the most important sector in the French economy.

The question of distribution has led to the greatest number of myths about France. In the field of agriculture there have been major steps to improve distribution. The field of retail distribution however is where the most revolutionary progress has been made in the past five years.

Although the number of retail outlets is still large[1] and is still just dominated by the department stores (the *Grands Magasins*, such as the *Galeries Printemps* and the *Nouvelles Galeries*), they will probably be overtaken this year by the *Hypermarchés*. (In 1971 the *Grands Magasins* had 927,000 square metres of floorspace, the *Hypermarchés*, 817,000 square metres.)[2]

It is these establishments, rather than the *Supermarchés*,

Table 12

LABOUR FORCE ACCORDING TO SECTORS
(As percentage of total)

	1966	1970	Change 1966–70
Agriculture	16·0	13·2	– 19·5
Industry (not including Construction and Public Works)	30·1	29·4	+ 1·5
Service Industries	53·9	57·4	+ 10·4

Source: *Cahier Français* (January, February 1972).

[1] As late as 1965, independent retailers, or associations of independents which accounted for 92 % of all outlets, were responsible for 8 % of the total turnover in distribution and employed seven-eighths of the salaried employees.
[2] However in 1971 the *Hypermarchés* had increased their floorspace by 25 %. This figure might have been larger had the *Préfets* given building permission in the case of every application.

which give France much of her American looks at the present time. In comparison with the *Grands Magasins* which are normally found in city centres, the *Hypermarchés* have, in nearly all cases, been built either on the edge of towns or in the open countryside where rents are very low. They employ few staff and concentrate almost exclusively on the sale of food. Lastly, with their low prices and with their vast car parks they attract the masses of motorised young people who live in the new housing estates.

Table 13

PERSONAL CONSUMPTION
(As a percentage of total consumption)
(Expressed in current francs)

	1950	Position	1959	Position	1968	Position
Food	40·1	1	32·8	1	27·2	1
Clothing	15·2	2	11·5	2	10·3	2
Drink	9·8	3	9·8	3	7·0	6
Energy + Upkeep Materials	4·9	4	6·6	4	6·3	7
Medical Products	4·7	5	6·2	5	8·8	3
Household Fittings – Furniture	4·1	6	2·1	9	2·3	10
Hotels, Cafés, Restaurants	3·1	7	2·6	8	3·5	8
Automobiles	2·7	8	5·8	6	7·5	5
Public Transport	2·4	9	2·1	9	1·8	12
Rent	2·2	10	4·8	7	8·1	4
Tobacco + Matches	2·4	11	2·1	9	1·7	14
Books, Journals, Newspapers	1·3	12	1·6	12	1·8	12
Personal Hygiene	1·3	12	1·4	13	2·2	11
Entertainment	0·8	13	0·9	15	0·8	15
Toys, etc.	0·7	14	1·9	11	2·5	9
Radio, Television, Cameras	0·4	15	1·0	14	1·3	14
Sport + Camping	0·1	15	0·3	16	0·6	16

Source: *Consommation* (April/September 1970).

AGRICULTURE

Agriculture has always been France's main industry, and in joining the European Economic Community she hoped to become the Granary of Europe. But, France has faced many difficulties in this area. Apart from the fundamental problem of specialisation, that is, too much concentration on cereals for too long, followed by a belated attempt to increase the production of beef, the main difficulties have been the lack of mechanisation of farming and the large numbers of small farming units in the country. Of late a further problem (which will prove an advantage as the older farmers fade away) has been the increasingly ageing population engaged in agriculture in France.

The main problems are amply demonstrated by the fact that only in 1956 did mechanisation in agriculture make any headway (see the table below) and only during the course of the Third Plan did output reach the targets planned by the State.

Table 14

MECHANISATION OF AGRICULTURE

Years	Tractors	Combined Harvesters	Mechanised Ploughs	Harvesters
1938	35,000	200	6,000	1,000
1945	37,000	—	—	1,500
1946	44,000	250	6,100	2,000
1947	54,000	310	8,100	3,500
1948	68,000	1,610	13,400	5,000
1949	95,000	2,700	20,800	7,500
1950	120,000	3,800	24,800	10,000
1951	142,000	4,975	28,000	12,000
1952	165,000	7,300	32,600	17,000
1953	195,000	10,500	38,300	22,300
1954	230,000	12,500	44,800	28,000
1955	270,000	15,000	52,000	32,600
1956	335,000	18,000	63,500	38,200
1957	425,000	23,000	80,700	45,000
1958	535,000	34,000	104,000	52,000
1959	625,000	42,000	120,000	58,000
1960	680,000	50,000	161,000	70,000
1961	750,000	57,000	195,000	75,000
1962	900,000	75,000	250,000	85,000
1963	957,000	85,000	300,000	95,000
1964	1,010,000	97,000	340,000	98,000
1965	1,050,000	110,000	400,000	104,500

Apart from direct intervention by the State intended to change the structure of agriculture (discussed below), the main weapon used to improve efficiency and productivity has been the system of maintained prices as adopted by the European

Economic Community (though French price levels were originally quite modest).

In the case of the increase in the quantity of machinery used by farmers, it is difficult to imagine that the success noted since 1956 would have been achieved without the formation of co-operatives. In turn, such associations would have been difficult to form without the financial support of the State. Thus the State did give financial support to co-operatives which would buy and use machinery. Equally, financial help was given to associations which bought up and redistributed land. These associations which are known as the S.A.F.E.R.s (*Sociétés d'Aménagement Foncier et d'Etablissement Rural*), had, up to the end of 1967, bought up about 230,000 hectares of land, and had given back 143,000 hectares, thus increasing the size of the receiving holdings by about a third on average. Unfortunately, although this form of intervention concerned 15% of all land transactions, it only covered 7% of usable land. Further, the Vedel Report (page 42, *Première partie*) bitterly criticised the anti-social effect of these operations. The Report maintained that instead of buying-up large holdings and giving them to smallholders, the tendency has been to buy up many small-holdings and to re-let a reduced number of these holdings. Further, any improved efficiency has tended to negatively affect neighbouring farms.

Possibly of greater social success has been the use of State intervention through the I.V.D.s (the *Indemnités Viagères de Départ*), to prematurely retire older farmers without them suffering any financial loss. The following record of numbers of retirements would seem to vindicate the social and material success of these operations.

Table 15

NUMBERS OF I.V.D.S PER YEAR
(As on 1 January each year)

1965	13,298
1966	32,279
1967	72,664
1968	107,390

Apart from operations of this nature, it would not be un-reasonable to assume that the massive exodus from the land in

France has been mainly due to low incomes caused by low prices for agricultural produce and by the small size of many French farms. The lower farm incomes when compared with the rising incomes of other social groups, appear even smaller.

Aid has also been given to associations which have attempted to organise the sale of farmers' produce on a collective basis.[1] Similarly, in its desire to improve the system of distribution of agricultural produce, the State has constructed *Marchés Gares* near the major centres of population in the country.

It seems that reforms in agriculture are most likely to succeed in France when the State actively associates itself with policy and reforms. One of these reforms was the decision, in 1966, to allow the *Crédit Agricole* to broaden its activities and to become a much more flexible type of farmers' bank.

In 1969, simultaneously with the devaluation of the franc and the decision of the government to increase the price of beef (as an encouragement to farmers to move from cereal growing into beef production)[2] and to reduce the price of animal foodstuffs, the famous Vedel Report was published concerning itself with the future of French agriculture.[3] This report, which has led to a furore among French farmers, sets out a host of figures. These do confirm the well-established fact that the percentage of the working population employed in agriculture has been falling[4] and that productivity has been rising. However, in France itself, despite the increasing population, the increase in food consumption has been slowing down. Between 1950 and 1960, the annual increase per person was on average 2·2%; between 1960 and 1970 it was only 1·55%. The Report naturally concluded that any extra demand would have to be generated from outside France, particularly among her partners of the Community, but expressed fears about France's competitive ability. Fortunately recent trade figures do not vindicate the fears expressed by the Vedel Commission[5] (see table, page 42). The uproar

---

[1] These associations are known as the *Sociétés d'Intérêt Collectif Agricole*.

[2] This was long overdue in view of the price support which had always been given to milk and cereal producers.

[3] *Le Rapport Vedel*, '*Perspectives à long terme de l'agriculture française 1968–1985*' (Self: Paris, 1969).

[4] The number of farmers fell from 1,400,000 in 1963 to 1,270,000 in 1967.

[5] The Report did concede that agricultural products as a percentage of French exports had risen.

caused among farmers by this Report was occasioned by the necessity, expressed in the study, to accelerate the exodus from the land between now and 1985. This statement, coming shortly after the admission that the prices of agricultural products had been falling by an average of one per cent per annum, was not acceptable to most farmers. Further, the study considered that the market support given by the State had only slowed down the fall in prices. It also pointed to the feeble (relative to that for cereal and milk production) price support for beef production in the Common Market. The Report concluded that France should seek means of creating new jobs for the desired accelerated exodus from the land and should encourage the creation of larger units of production in order to improve her competitive position.[1] Probably this study should have emphasised more a policy of greater support for increased prices in certain products such as beef, rather than concentrating so much on the exodus from the land, which will in any case take place due to the large number of persons employed in agriculture in France who are relatively old.

In the preparation of the current and Sixth National Plan, the French Government insisted that most of the financial aid for agriculture would be given to those farmers who organised themselves into associations. This re-emphasising of the F.O.R.M.A. (*Fonds d'Orientation et de Régularisation des Marchés Agricoles*) from 1969, showed that on 1 April of that year, organised groups/associations of farmers were responsible for the following percentages of total production:

	%
Fruits	50
Chickens	30
Eggs and beef	10
Pigs	8

However in 1969 only 300,000, that is one in six, belonged to such associations. This fact is highlighted by the penetration of the food market in France by such firms as B.S.N., Perrier, Unilever and Nestlé. Subsequently the agricultural committee working with the Plan considered that aid should only be given to the most organised and dynamic elements in French agriculture.

---

[1] It also suggested that by 1985, one third of the usable land in France should be returned to its natural state.

The committee was even more categoric in its wish that the associations of farmers should shoulder some of the financial responsibility of intervening in the market to maintain price levels. This desire was underlined by the increase in aid by the State for price support. In 1960 this aid had totalled 842 million francs; in 1965, 1800 millions; in 1967, 2879 millions; and in 1968, 4910 millions. Over the period 1965 to 1969, the State intervention had increased 3·3 times, and in 1969 constituted 37% of government help to agriculture compared with 25% four years earlier. The conclusion which one might draw from such a policy is that it has led to the creation of surpluses of produce that no one wants, whilst the incomes of farmers continue to fall. The type of selectivity of such price support is most unusual. During the period 1968–9, the percentages of the total price support were divided as follows:

	%
Cereals and beet	31·8+
Milk	13·3
Pork, chickens and eggs	1·0

Since, in 1968, 20% of French farmers were responsible for 60% of total agricultural output, most of the financial aid must have gone to the really large farmers who were producing surplus output.

Apart from the suggestions put forward by the members of the Plan and by the *Rapport Vedel*, other individuals and associations have put forward somewhat different solutions. The President of the Association of Wheat Growers, M. J. Deleau, has proposed the introduction of a quota system for wheat producers. The *Jeunes Agriculteurs* want to introduce a new scale of prices, much more favourable to beef production than the present system; a tax system for producers of surpluses; indemnities for poor farmers and a more regional system of State credits for machinery and equipment.[1]

A former President of the *Fonds d'Orientation et de Régularisation des Marchés Agricoles*, M. P. Lelong, has been most critical

[1] More recently part of this proposal has been accepted by the Government by the introduction of initial grants of about 22,000 francs to young farmers setting up in poor agricultural regions.

of the present system. In an article published in *Le Monde*[1] in 1970, he pointed out that the present chaos in French agriculture is due to the fact that according to the agreements made in Brussels in 1966 and 1967, the support for the market comes from public funds, whereas originally the plan in France had been that the associations of producers should themselves be financially responsible for removing the surpluses from the market. Such regional associations would, of course, have to be supervised by a government commissioner. Thus, M. Lelong is asking for a greater degree of responsibility from French and other European farmers. Basically he is saying that if the European Economic Community is willing to maintain high prices for agricultural produce, then the farmers themselves should pay the price for removing surpluses from the market.

Lastly it should not be ignored that the State, in creating in 1962 the *Associations d'Agriculteurs*, had hoped that they would not only assume the responsibility (upon receipt of public funds) of controlling the market, but also organise a more effective system of distribution for their produce. The appearance of the *Rapport Lenoir* (which studied three sectors, fruit, vegetables and eggs) following the publication of the *Rapport Vedel*, caused consternation in government circles. In only one case, that of the organisation of spring vegetables in Brittany, could the Report note real efficiency and success in distribution. Such an observation is surprising when one considers that the Report found that these associations were nevertheless responsible for distributing 40% of all fruits and vegetables, between 40 and 50% of all chickens and about 25% of all eggs!

Again, the success of the co-operative societies in Brittany was referred to when the study concluded that some associations were 'straw' organisations, intent purely on receiving public finance. Such a finding would tend to reinforce M. Lelong's wish that such associations be controlled by government commissioners.

In some areas, there was a positive profusion of associations, themselves too small in size and competing against one another.[2]

[1] P. Lelong, *Marchés agricoles et responsabilité des Producteurs* in *Le Monde* (27 August 1970).

[2] Two such examples were the Drôme, where 21 such associations were responsible for fruit and vegetables; and the Vaucluse with 19. This meant that three or four groups would compete in the one canton.

The actions of the administration in legalising so many associations was also criticised. Further, no distinction was made between very wealthy and poor associations, and there was evidence of fraud – reaching a level of 40–50% in the case of the fruit and vegetable sector.

As in other studies, the *Rapport Lenoir* concluded that aid should continue to be given to organised groups of farmers but that they should assume some financial responsibility for the removal of surplus produce from the market.

Tables 16–17

FRENCH FIRMS BY INDUSTRY: COMPETITIVE RANKING:
PROFITABILITY AND SIZE: 1970

	Profitability	Turnover (*in million francs*)
(i) *Car Industry*	%	
(A) B.M.W.	15·4	2,564
(F) Peugeot S.A.	14·7	7,715
(A) Daimler-Benz	13·6	17,680
(A) Volkswagen	8·4	23,913
(R.-U.) B.L.M.C.	0·2	13,497
(ii) *Chemical Industry*	%	
(F) Usine Kuhlmann	13·3	6,336
(A) B.A.S.F.	9·4	15,931
(R.-U.) I.C.I.	9·2	19,333
(A) Hoechst	9·0	16,779
(A) Bayer	7·7	16,854
(F) Rhône-Poulenc	7·5	11,027
(P.-B.) A.K.Z.O.	7·5	11,132
(iii) *Textiles*	%	
(R.-U.) Courtaulds	10·3	8,720
(R.-U.) Coats Patons	7·4	3,939
(R.-U.) English Calico	6·9	2,010
(F) Agache-Willot	3·3	1,861
(R.-U.) Carrington-Viyella	0·4	1,736
(iv) *Steel*	%	
(F) Usinor	14·7	5,304
(L) Arbedé	13·9	4,055
(A) Hoechst	8·5	6,885
(P.-B.) Hoogovens	8·0	3,264
(A) Thyssen	7·4	16,477
(F) Wendel-Sidélor	7·2	5,905
(A) Mannesmann	6·8	11,150
(R.-U.) British Steel	1·0	19,267

	Profitability	*Turnover* (*in million francs*)
(v) *Mechanical Industry*	%	
(S) S.K.F.	8·8	5,087
(R.-U.) G.K.N.	8·8	6,415
(A) M.A.N.	8·7	5,005
(F) Creusot-Loire	8·1	3,074
(A) K.H.D.	5·8	4,573
(A) G.H.H.	3·2	9,607
(R.-U.) Vickers	2·6	2,290
(vi) *Electronics*	%	
(R.-U.) Thorn	20·0	4,529
(R.-U.) Rank	19·3	2,474
(R.-U.) Plessey	10·7	2,747
(S) Ericsson	10·6	3,378
(F) Groupe C.G.E.	9·5	8,610
(A) A.E.G.	7·7	11,408
(A) Siemens	7·0	17,814
(I) Olivetti	6·1	4,120
(P.-B.) Philips	6·0	23,057
(F) Thomson	6·0	6,615
(vii) *Distribution*	%	
(F) Carrefour	30·2	1,448
(R.-U.) Marks and Spencer	25·4	5,508
(F) Casino	23·7	1,867
(R.-U.) Tesco Stores	21·0	3,159
(A) Kaufhof	16·0	5,618
(A) Karstadt	15·0	6,373
(viii) *Banking*		*Deposits*
(R.-U.) Barclays Bank		77,018
(R.-U.) National Westminster		71,879
(F) B.N.P.		60,642
(A) Deutsche Bank		58,288
(F) Crédit Lyonnais		54,141
(I) Banca Com. italiana		51,717
(R.-U.) Midland Bank		49,185

Source: *Expansion*, No. 45 (Autumn 1971).

5 The Environment

THE FRENCH REGIONAL QUESTION

When M. J. F. Gravier's work, *Paris et le Désert Français* (itself originally a roneotyped paper which circulated in the French Treasury) was published by Flammarion in 1947, the stage was set for a gradual intensification of an environmental battle in France, dating back to 1790, the regional conflict. Indeed most environmental questions may be reduced to the question of the intensive concentration in and around Paris and a few other centres, to the detriment of most regions which were well-balanced in population and economic distribution in the eighteenth century.

But this question, as the late and illustrious editor of *Le Canard Enchaîné*, Morvan Lebesque, poignantly wrote in 1970,[1] shortly before his untimely death, is essentially an administrative economic and political question. It is not simply a result of the fact that the economic forces tended to concentrate themselves around Paris, in the North and in Lorraine (together with a few urban centres such as Lyon), and that the road and rail systems tended to radiate from the national capital; but it is also a result of the additional fact that since 1790, but particularly since February 1800, the whole administrative apparatus of the regions has been centred on Paris. Only in April 1969, and more recently in 1972, have efforts really been made to ameliorate this situation. Even these efforts have not been free from the taint of corporatism which Jacques Duclos had already foreseen and criticised in 1963.[2]

Thus any understanding of economic help for the regions, of cultural centres and of pollution does first necessitate an understanding of the incredible concentration of regional administrative and financial control in Paris and the gradual moves to change this state of affairs.

[1] M. Lebesque, *Comment peut-on être Breton?* (du Seuil, 1970).
[2] J. Duclos, *Gaullisme, technocratie, corporatisme* (Editions Sociales, 1963).

The Regions: Background to the Problem

As Gravier himself has recently pointed out, it would be wrong to assume that the importance of the French regions ceased with the peak of the monarchy.[1] On the contrary, as just mentioned, he gives the example of the Languedoc, which like some other regions, levied taxes both for royal and their own use, and due to the good reputation of their management and financial standing, the royal government was able to borrow money with the backing of the province, a thing which it could not have done using its own name![2]

One of the aims of the French Revolution had been to give power and representation to the regions. Unfortunately the former provinces disappeared in 1790 and were replaced by the departments (*Départements*). In 1800, prefects (*Préfets*) were placed at the head of each department, helped simply by a consultative general Council (*Conseil Général Consultatif*), chosen from certain carefully defined lists of personalities.

The situation evolved a little when in 1871 the *Conseil Général* was made a deliberative organ and was enabled to vote the budget prepared by the *Préfet*. Also, a *Commission Départementale* was set up, to be composed of between four and seven members, to be elected annually by the *Conseil Général*, with the task of controlling the *Préfet*'s actions between sessions.[3]

After a brief flirtation with regionalism through the nomination and work of the *Commissaires de la République* (the sons of the Resistance) immediately after the last war, there was a return to the institutions of the *Départements* and the *Communes*. Thus the administrative structure remained until the changes of the 1960s and the 1970s.

Since 1945 however certain economic bodies evolved (though very frequently under the control and/or supervision of the *Préfet*) and certain economic incentives were devised. This was inevitable in view of the accelerated growth of the Paris region and the depopulation of Brittany, the south-west and the centre.

[1] J. F. Gravier, *La Question régionale* (Flammarion, 1970), page 21.

[2] A very detailed account of the regional development in France is given by M. Bourjol, *Les Institutions régionales de 1789 à nos jours* (Berger-Levrault, 1969).

[3] The *Députés*, *Conseilleurs Généraux*, Senators and Mayors of *Chefs-Lieux* could not be elected to this body.

The birth of the equivalent of the British Town and Country Planning Act had taken place during the life of the Vichy régime, in the form of the *Délégation à l'Equipement National.* After the War, this had been merged with the Ministry of Reconstruction. In 1950, M. Claudius-Petit, Minister for Construction, had written a brochure entitled, *Pour un plan national d'aménagement du territoire.* He also created a fund to provide finance for industrial zones in the defavourised regions, *Le Fonds National d'Aménagement du Territoire.* This was the first official acknowledgement of the regional problem which was translated into concrete terms.

The next moves were unofficial and consisted mainly of the setting up by businessmen and other persons of *Comités d'Expansion.* Mendès-France recognised the importance of these bodies and decreed, in 1954, that they were to be consulted by the *Préfets* and other officials. The following year, 1955, the first restrictions on industrialisation in the Paris region were introduced, and were complemented in the same year by the introduction of special incentives for particularly defavourised regions, *Primes Spéciales d'Equipement* in the *Zones Critiques.*

The first recognition of the regions was the designation, in 1956, of twenty-two (later reduced to twenty-one) *Régions de Programme.* The logical sequence of this creation, in such a highly centralised State as France, was naturally the nomination of individuals who would co-ordinate the aid for such regions. In 1959 the creation of a form of Super Prefect, the *Préfet Coordonnateur,* was first proposed. This individual was to apply both the regional plan and the government's economic policy. The uproar caused by this proposal, both among the existing *corps préfectoral* (who saw their own demotion) and among those who saw a greater degree of centralisation as the government's intention, led to the postponement of the nomination of these Super Prefects until 1961.

At national level, proof of the increasing consciousness of the gravity of the regional problem was seen in the creation in 1964 of the C.N.A.T., *Commission Nationale d'Aménagement du Territoire,* as part of the central planning organisation. There is also an executive body, the *Comité Interministériel de l'Aménagement du Territoire,* made up of the ministers having responsibility in the regional field. These ministers meet regularly under the chairmanship of the Prime Minister and compare their views with those of the *Délégation Générale*, which is directly controlled by the Prime Minister, and whose task is to ensure that the administration follows the directives of the Plan. Since 1964 the central budget has been regionalised, and the *Délégation Générale* is associated with the elaboration of the budget.

It appeared that the suspicions of those who had seen the creation of larger administrative regions as a greater concentration of central power were realised when, in 1964, the government decreed that henceforth the *Préfet* alone exercised the powers of the State (*le seul dépositaire des pouvoirs de l'Etat*) in the regions. Eventually the prefects were given the power to decide on the financial incentives to be given to the regions (the *Primes de Développement et d'Adaptation Industrielle*). Further, the central authorities had become increasingly suspicious of the *Comités d'Expansion* because of their close links with private enterprise. The upshot was the creation in 1964 of the C.O.D.E.R.s, the *Commissions de Développement Economique Régional.*[1]

Again any further illusions regarding a possible reduction of central control were removed by the government declaration of 1968, reasserting that the *Préfets* were the economic and administrative delegates of the government in the regions (for financial projects, they do of course have to seek the advice of the *Trésorier-Payeur Général de la Région*). By 1966 it had been

[1] Thus, in order of administrative importance, four types of regional organisations exist:

1. The *Préfets de Région*. Apart from the responsibilities already defined, they also prepare the 'regional slice' of the national plan and control the S.D.R.s.

2. The C.O.D.E.R.s. These are strictly consultative bodies consisting of representatives of employers, trade unions, etc. They can only meet on the invitation of the *Préfet de Région*, who services their activities!

3. The *Sociétés d'Aménagement*. These are mixed economy societies in which the State normally has a majority holding. The most notable of these is the *Compagnie d'Aménagement du Bas-Rhône et du Languedoc*.

4. The S.D.R.s, *Sociétés de Développement Régional*. These are corporations set up mainly on the initiative of local businessmen (normally banks). They benefit from two advantages, the State guarantees the dividend paid to the stockholders, and they are able to launch bond issues.

5. In 1966 the *Bureaux d'Industrialisation* (*Associations pour l'Expansion Industrielle*) were created. They were placed in areas such as the Nord, to reconvert worn-out old industries. They are composed exclusively of industrialists and act as intermediaries for the old and new industries.

realised that any even spread of regional aid was fairly pointless and that *Métropoles d'Equilibre – Communautés Urbaines,* should be set up both for economic reasons and also, culturally, to attempt to give a counter-weight to the pull of Paris. Some of the most notable of these centres are Lyon-St. Etienne and Bordeaux-Toulouse. It is perhaps in this field where the hope for the future of the regions in France lies – although these great communities are finding difficulty in finding the necessary finance for their projects.

Nevertheless there are signs that these communities are beginning (apart from the construction of the *Maisons de la Culture* throughout France) to counteract the pull of Paris. The cultural renaissance of Lyon (particularly in the field of opera) and the creation in 1972 of a T.N.P. (*Théâtre National Populaire*) in that city is most important. Again in Lyon, there are now plans to set up a national banking centre there. The increase in the establishment of foreign banks in Lyon in recent years would give strength to such a centre.

By 1969 de Gaulle himself was aware of the regional question and made a declaration to this effect, in March, in Lyon. In April he inadvertently linked the vote on the regional issue with the question of merging the *Senate* with the *Conseil Economique et Social* – the vote was of course rejected. His proposals are nevertheless worth examining. He saw the region as a *Collectivité Territoriale* with a mission to '*Contribuer au développement économique, social et culturel, ainsi qu'à l'aménagement de la partie correspondante du territoire national*'. He suggested (and this was really crucially important) that some national taxes should be transferred to the regions and that they would enjoy the same financial rights as the *Départements*.[1] The *Conseils Régionaux* were to be corporative in quality and content and not democratically elected whilst the *Préfet's* place was reconfirmed in the regional framework.

Finally, in January 1972, the long-awaited regional reforms were made public.[2] They reinforced the authority of the regional *Préfet* and increased the State financial aid, particularly for the

[1] The necessity for such action was stressed by Alain Vernholes in *Le Monde* (15 April 1969) when he pointed out that those localities which had not enough finances of their own had to cover 60 % of infra-structural needs through loans and 20 % from State subsidies.

[2] To be introduced in 1973.

industrialisation of the west, the eastern frontier regions and the conversion of the coal-mining areas. The one change concerns medium-sized towns which will receive greater aid, formerly only given to main metropolitan centres.

One significant change in the financial aid to the private sector is the merging of the different levels of incentives, P.D.R.s, *Primes de Développement Régionales*, into one, although different areas will still qualify for different levels of financial aid!

As before, the direct subsidies, given by the F.D.E.S. (*Fonds de Développement et Social*) and the F.I.A.T. (*Fonds d'Intervention pour l'Aménagement du Territoire*), will continue to occupy an important position.

In strict economic terms, what do the new incentives mean and what are the financial possibilities at the disposal of the regions, the departments and the communes? First, the State has agreed to transfer one financial right to the regions, the revenue derived from the payments for driving licences. In its totality, in 1972, this meant 50 million francs (excluding the Paris region); in reality, on the basis of the motorised public, some regions will be much richer than others. There already exist some forty minor taxes (including the revenue from the sales of dog licences!) which the regions and localities may use. In their quantitative effect they are small. They may impose a local infra-structure tax on the existing local taxes, a limit or 'plafond' being fixed to these tax increases. Thus in the most important region, Rhône-Alpes, the limit would be 110 million francs; in a medium-sized region like Picardie, it would be 40 million francs; in a sparsely populated region like the Limousin, it would be 20 million francs. If the regions use all the possibilities at their disposal, they could in total acquire a maximum of 1000 million francs. This sum is four times that available to the F.I.A.T.[1] Apart from the taxes and subsidies, the regions may float loans, as did the City and Region of Marseille in 1972. However if regions use all possible taxes, this would amount to only 5% of total disposable regional resources. The new incen-

---

[1] The possibility of having recourse to new forms of taxation is demonstrated by the following increases in existing local taxes by the following cities in 1972 to cover increased expenditure: Besançon, 35 %; Dijon, 14 %; Limoges, 22 %; Nancy, 30 %; Nice, 20 %; Orléans, 25 %; Reims, 17 %; Strasbourg, 30 %; and Tours, 18·5 %.

tives which are very much the former ones in a slightly new guise are as follows:

(i) The former *Primes d'Adaptation* and the *Primes de Développement* are replaced by the one P.D.R., *Prime de Développement Régional*. As before, the amounts involved do vary from region to region. There is nevertheless one departure from former practices. In the case of most of the regions concerned, the west, the eastern frontier regions and the 'conversion' areas, coal-mining, steel and textile industrial areas, the new incentives will last for the duration of the current and Sixth Plan (1972–5). However certain towns, such as Dieppe and Angers, have also been included in the regions qualifying for aid – but only for the first eighteen months of the current Plan.

The incentives are:

(a) 15% of total investments for setting up a new factory;
(b) 12% for extensions to a factory;
(c) In certain areas – in the west and elsewhere, the incentives may amount to 25% of investment costs. Also the government reserves the right to give the maximum incentives to certain medium-sized towns.

As already indicated, the *Préfet*'s powers have been extended. They are empowered to examine all investment programmes of more than 5 million francs in value. All programmes of more than 10 million francs in value will be examined centrally by the government which reserves the right to give any incentive varying from 0 to 25% towards the costs of any such projects.

(ii) Incentives for decentralisation and service industries.

These incentives are fairly novel. There are three types of incentive in this category:

(a) 10% for administrative purposes
(b) 15% for research and study purposes
and
(c) 20% for such operations involving the transfer of headquarters.

Hitherto, as the D.A.T.A.R. had indicated in 1969, and as M. de Castelbajac has shown in a study consecrated to European regional aid,[1] the volume of State aid devoted to regional development in France has been poor. (For 1969–72, 500 million francs per annum; United Kingdom, 5000 million

[1] *Documentation Française*, June 1972.

francs per annum.) Further, with the exception of such metropolitan growth points as the areas around Lyon, Marseille,
Nice, and a few others, the Paris region continues to grow (the
only notable variation has been the fact, as in the case of
London, that the centre of the city has been depopulated,
1962, 2,790,000 inhabitants; 1968, 2,591,000 inhabitants).

It is too early to judge whether the new regional measures
decided upon in France will reverse this trend. It is possible
that the exodus from the land will continue, but that the regional
metropolitan areas will grow at least as quickly as the Paris
region. For the moment the regional differences in incomes in
France still remain.

Table 18

GROWTH OF URBAN CENTRES, 1962–70
(Percentage growth)

Toulouse	+ 20·8
Marseille – Aix – Berre	+ 20·3
Lyon – Grenoble – St. Etienne	+ 16·3
Bordeaux	+ 14·2
Strasbourg	+ 13·3
Nantes – Saint-Nazaire	+ 13·2
Nancy – Metz	+ 13·0
Lille	+ 9·4
Paris Region	+ 11·2

THE ENVIRONMENT AND THE ECONOMY

France did not create its Ministry of the Environment until 1971.
Environmental problems, especially where their solution could
be linked with the economic rejuvenation of a region, had been
of importance for many years. The first national park, the *Parc
National de la Vanoise*, had been created in 1963, partly with
the aim of saving a beautiful region and partly with the aim of
giving economic aid to the peripheral areas of the park.[1]

A year earlier, in 1962, the famous *Loi Malraux* enabled
protection orders to be placed on whole districts of outstanding
architectural importance, rather than on individual monuments

[1] There are (in 1972) four national parks (a further two are planned) and nine
regional natural parks.

as had hitherto been the case.[1] Also under Malraux, an impetus was given to the construction of over twenty *Maisons de la Culture*. Many of these cultural centres (for example the one at Grenoble) are outstanding centres and often contain cinemas, theatres, exhibition halls, restaurants and even nurseries where parents may leave their children whilst they watch a film or play. These centres have done much to revive the provinces.

In the field of the protection of ancient monuments, it is worth remembering that the fabric of the churches of France is maintained by the State since they are regarded as monuments of national architectural and historical interest.

As the appendix at the end of this section illustrates, French environmental policy is not new. Laws have existed since 1914 and particularly since 1930 to protect the environment. Further, with the creation of the first national park in 1963, it was intended that the division of the park into three areas, *Réserves Intégrales* (for scientists and scholars), *Le Parc* (for visitors) and the *Zone Périphérique* where a socio-economic stimulus was given, would encourage the localities to give up their properties to the State in exchange for economic help on the one hand, and associate themselves with the park on the other.

The creation of the *Ministère de l'Environnement* in 1971 has underlined the importance of the environmental problem. It is however through the simultaneous creation of the F.I.A.N.E. (*Fonds d'Intervention et d'Action pour la Nature et l'Environnement*) that the Ministry itself has been very active. This body seeks to encourage local industries and authorities to associate themselves with environmental projects. It gives financial help to experimental projects, helps to create and equip national parks, educates young people in specially created centres, saves parks in urban centres, helps to restore damaged countryside and helps to prevent pollution created by new industries. To date its most important realisations have been the cleaning up of the Lake of Annecy and the safeguarding of important sections of the Forest of Fontainebleau for Parisians. In addition, it plans to clean up the Lakes of Le Bourget and Nantua.

It was to be expected that the real teeth for environmental

---

[1] This Law has been crucial in enabling such districts as the Marais in Paris and the Vieux Lyon to be gradually restored.

policy in France would be given to the F.I.A.N.E. In July 1972 a further 28 million francs were given to this organisation. Of this sum about 9 millions were to be used to acquire green spaces for municipalities (including new towns) – in January 1972 a census of all green spaces on the edge of towns was organised. About 10 million francs would be used to extend the operation, started in 1970, to clean up rivers,[1] and the remaining amount would be used to remove waste.

In February 1971 the Ministry of the Environment organised an operation within a radius of 120 kilometres round Lyon, intended to recuperate car carcases and have them disposed of in a specially designated centre. A year later, 37,710 car bodies had been disposed of at a cost of 1,500,000 francs. In each case, the person who disposed of the vehicle received 30 francs.

This operation is the beginning of a policy intended to make the protection of the environment economically as well as aesthetically attractive.

The problem of the disposal of car bodies is a subject of growing concern in France. In 1964, 250,000 cars were no longer fit for use; in 1972, the estimated figure was 1,200,000. Thus, following the experiment conducted in the region of Lyon, it was decided, in July 1972, that in future the setting up of car dumps would have to be authorised by the *Préfet* in each *département*. Also it was agreed that in future the fine for abandoning a car would be between 600 and 1000 francs. The task of finding the culprits would be made more easy by placing on a central computer of all the numbers and details of driving licences which would be linked with the car manufacturers' number.

In the same field of cars, France, like Western Germany, has undertaken most important and beneficial legislation regarding the lead content of petrol. In 1972 the permissible maximum level of lead was 0·64 grams per litre. By 1 January 1976, it is planned to reduce this to 0·45 grams per litre.[2] The environmental problem then is being solved in France in two ways, through Government finance for environmental projects and by making environmental protection economically attractive to private individuals.

[1] To date three rivers have been treated, now a further six will be cleaned.
[2] France has also introduced similar legislation for the sulphur content of domestic fuel oils.

HOUSING

France has made much effort in the field of housing (as in the field of manufacturing) to make good the stagnation of the interwar years and to repair the war losses (11% of all the nation's homes had been lost during the course of the hostilities). As in many other fields, the major responsibility for this rebuilding has been undertaken by the State.[1] It is perhaps this factor that explains (as in other countries) the relative monotony and sometimes the sheer ugliness of much of France's housing construction. The lesson of this state of affairs appeared to have been learned, when in 1972 it was decided that extra resources would be allocated to 'improved' municipal housing projects.

If friends of France constantly criticise the mediocre appearance or the ugliness of so much of the country's housing, there has nevertheless been a considerable improvement in the amenities offered by new homes. Equally, the number of rooms per home has increased: 3·3 in 1961, 3·6 in 1963 and 3·7 in 1967. The increase in the number of homes with amenities is clearly seen from table 19.

The rents of homes in France have increased since 1958, and substantially in recent years. The rents of old houses are controlled by a Law of 1 September 1948. There have been rent increases among this category of homes, but they have been substantially less than for new houses and flats. Indeed the rapid increase in the rents of new homes in recent years most probably explains the sudden recent upsurge in house-buying in France – a phenomenon practically unknown in the country ten years ago. The most recent sign of this movement is the decision by the S.C.I.C. – the branch of the *Caisse des Dépôts et Consignations* – to sell 64% of the homes on which building had started. During the period 1954–70, 77% of the homes constructed had been rented. Another interesting change being made by the same society is shown in the fall in the number of homes being built in the Paris region (54% in 1954 and 38% in 1971).[2] Thus

[1] Even during the period 1971–73, it is expected that the State will directly or indirectly help to finance most housing construction.

[2] Expressed as a percentage of the total number of homes completed by the society.

there are the beginnings of the movement of economic forces back to the regions.

Table 19

QUALITY OF HOUSING
(As a percentage of the total number of homes)

	Without running water	Without bath or shower	Without internal W.C.	Without central heating
1962	18·9	60·6	60·0	80·0
1963	17·2	63·6	60·0	80·0
1965	12·7	57·5	53·0	76·0
1967	9·5	51·3	47·0	71·0

Source: *Consommation 1970* numbers 2 and 3.

In general in 1967 the rents of homes built since the war (non H.L.M.) were 2·5 times higher than those for older homes. For the H.L.M., the difference only amounted to 50%. A clearer indication of the important place being taken by housing in the French household budget is the position in the list of expenses of the average household. In 1959 rents took up 4·8% of household expenses and occupied seventh place; in 1968 they took up 8% of expenses and were listed fourth.

Table 20

AVERAGE ANNUAL RENT IN FRANCS

	Old		New H.L.M.		New – Non H.L.M.	
	1963	1967	1963	1967	1963	1967
Rural Communes	535	823	—	—	—	—
Towns with less than 100,000 inhabitants	796	1248	1109	1801	2073	3109
Towns with more than 100,000 inhabitants	872	1216	1245	1809	2352	3458
PARIS REGION	1015	1467	1436	3050	3607	3921

Source: *Consommation 1970* numbers 2 and 3.

The most famous type of subsidised home in France is the H.L.M. (*Habitations à Loyer Modéré*). Until 1964 the groups constructing these homes also produced homes for people whose needs were very great and who had demonstrated their need. These homes were known as the L.O.C.E.C.O.S. (*Logements Economiques et Familiaux*). In the same year these organisations started to build homes for people who would be willing to pay higher rents for homes of higher quality. These homes, known as the I.L.N. (*Immeubles à Loyer Normal*) will henceforth receive greater support from the H.L.M. organisations.

The H.L.M. organisations are public establishments which are set up by decree following a request by the *Conseil Général*, a group of *Communes* or a municipality. They are responsible for both the construction and management of properties and are governed by boards of which a third of the members are nominated by the relevant local authorities.

At first these organisations have funds which they are given by local authorities and/or individuals.

The desire by Frenchmen to own their own homes has increased rapidly in recent years. Building societies as are known in Britain are of relatively recent origin (although a Law permitting their formation had been passed many years ago) and have experienced a number of rather embarrassing scandals in recent years.[1] These upheavals have coincided with the desire of the government to enlarge the scope of the banks, but again more recently to control finances used for construction more carefully. Thus, already since 1965, the *Crédit Foncier* had been used to help the banks to grant loans to home-buyers.[2]

In December 1971 the government decided to reform the whole system. As from 1972, the P.S.D.s have been abolished. They were replaced by the P.I.C.s (*Prêts Immobiliers Conventionnés*). These new loans are much more generous than anything that had hitherto been known in France. They cover up to 80 % of the cost of a home, may be of a duration of 25 years,

---

[1] One such example was the case of the *Garantie Foncière*.

[2] These loans, known as the P.S.D.s (*Prêts Spéciaux différés*) based on a Law dated 24 December 1963, covered between 45–50 % of the cost of the home. The average rate of interest in 1971 was 9 %, and on average 45,000 homes a year were built using this system.

and carry an average annual rate of interest of 8·24%. In March 1972 the *Crédit Lyonnais* and the B.N.P. (*Banque Nationale de Paris*) both signed agreements with the *Crédit Foncier*, allowing them to offer these facilities to their clients. Immediately other financial institutions made competitive moves to offer more advantageous terms to their customers.

France has also set up a national institution endowed with great independence and with funds amounting to 300 million francs (plus a further 8 millions for administering its central headquarters and local branches). This organisation is the A.N.A.H. (*Agence Nationale pour l'Amélioration de l'Habitat*).

The hitherto somewhat pessimistic view of construction in France should not lead one to imagine that the point of no return has been reached. In September 1965 the Ministry of Construction sent a circular to the *préfectures* asking that the 'siting, colours, forms and materials' used should be taken into account when issuing building licences. This request is now being reviewed in a more energetic fashion; and, linked with the increased finances for quality subsidised building, the efforts of the Ministry of the Environment, and the plans to restrict the height of new buildings in Paris and even to extend the perimeter around historic buildings in which no high buildings may be constructed, it is clear that a change is slowly taking place in French attitudes to building. The slowness of the change has not, alas, prevented the approval of the proposed construction of the motorway on the left bank of the Seine in Paris – a proposal which caused a Lille architect to sketch Notre-Dame with traffic circulating through two of the Western portals, past a notice on which was printed, 'please do not use your horns during the service'.

As in many fields of the French economy, it is more frequent that projects are likely to be successfully completed when the State actively associates itself with their realisation. Again, this can be done through a hundred per cent or through a partial participation.

Although France has not produced a series of 'new' towns[1]

---

[1] Recently, a number of new towns have been created in the Paris region. An important new town, L'Isle d'Abeau, is currently being built for 100,000 inhabitants in an area between Lyon and Grenoble. Another town is Vaudreuil, near Rouen.

in the British sense of the expression, she has legal instruments at her disposal which have encouraged some control over random housebuilding. These instruments are the Z.U.P. (*Zones à Urbaniser Priorité*) and the Z.A.D. (*Zones d'Aménagement Différé*). Local authorities may declare areas where development is imminent – Z.U.P.s – and all development of more than 100 units must take place within this zone. The State and/or the local authority has the prior right to acquire land in such an area. Further, within four years of such an area being declared a Z.U.P., owners of the land must first offer it for sale to the State and/or local authority. In order to avoid speculation taking place close to the Z.U.P.s, the State and/or local authorities may declare adjacent areas Z.A.D.s. In such areas the State and/or local authority have priority over any other buyers.

Some of the Z.U.P.s (especially the one at Toulouse – the Mirail) have been striking and homogeneous. At the same time, the example of the Z.U.P.s has led the State to undertake very large purchases of land and to become a partner in very large recreational projects such as *La Grande Motte* in the Roussillon and the current development on the coast of Aquitaine. One of the major aims of these projects is to diversify the economy and to bring employment to these regions.

CONCLUSION: THE ENVIRONMENT

In the narrow field of pollution, France is taking some active and constructive steps to find solutions to her problems, but this progress has not affected the bulk of pollution which manifests itself in the many unsightly buildings constructed since 1945.

In the field of urban planning, the whittling away of the laws – dating back to 1911 – due to the constant use of exceptions (*Dérogations*) which have allowed so many monstrosities to be built, leads one to conclude that France cannot be said to have any effective urban planning any more! Further, unlike some other European countries, there is no general education in architecture in the schools and on television. Apart from the existence of laudable conservation groups, whose interests lie in the field of older architecture, one is forced to conclude that here is no appreciation of the place of architecture in France.

This conclusion is supported by the fact that only in 1972 did the public in Paris awaken to the fact that the plans for the skyscrapers at Montparnasse and La Défense had been approved a decade earlier – in 1972 they were almost fully constructed!

Table 21

HOUSING: HOMES COMPLETED 1966–72
(In hundreds of thousands)

Note: During this period, an average of over 400,000 homes have been completed each year. The aim for 1972 is 500,000.

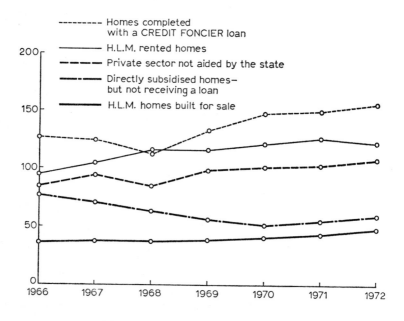

The insensitivity of modern France to architecture is matched only by her insensitivity to the hoardings which continue to disfigure her beautiful landscape. France appears to be in the process of adopting all that is worst in North America.

APPENDIX

French Laws – and the Environment

1. *Journal Officiel.* 4 January 1914.
   Law concerning the reparation of nuisances.
2. *Journal Officiel.* 4 May 1930.
   Delegation of powers to mayors and *préfets* in the prevention of nuisances.
3. Law for the Protection (2 May 1930) of natural monuments and sites of artistic, historical, scientific, legendary or picturesque interest.
   Creation of the *Commission Supérieure des Sites*. (This Commission has classified over 5000 sites.)
4. Creation (27 November 1946) of the *Conseil National pour la Protection de la Nature*.
5. Law (22 July 1960) making possible the creation of national parks – effective as from 2 November 1961.
6. Decrees, 2 February 1971, and 2 April 1971, set up the Ministry of the Environment and the F.I.A.N.E.

6 The Management of the French Economy 1945–70.

It is practically impossible, in the case of France, to dissociate macro-economic policy from wider planning considerations and prices and incomes policies. It is relatively easy for the observer to conclude that different aims were pursued at different moments in time, and that fiscal and monetary means, planning, deficit budgetary policies and prices and incomes policies were adopted wherever it was considered that they would support the fulfilment of the aims of the moment. In the case of macro-policy, only at the end of the 1960s, and now in the 1970s, have Keynesian policies been consciously used.

In, for example, examining national planning, economists sometimes forget what the real aims of the first three plans were, and equally it is occasionally forgotten that fiscal and monetary policies were used to achieve the aims of the plans.

At all times, in France, fiscal policy has been heavily weighted in favour of indirect taxation. Since the introduction of a diversified value added tax, it has been considered that this form of taxation has been fair. However, recent studies carried out by some trade unions and by the French Treasury tend to dispute this fact. These studies will be referred to later in this chapter.

There has been a real reason for this emphasis on indirect taxation. This has been the relative efficiency of collecting such a tax, its immediate effect on prices and therefore on the economy. These facts contrast with the inefficiency of collection of direct taxes and the high level of evasion which has been notable in this field.

More important from the standpoint of social equality have been the high levels of the social security taxes and the equally generous level of certain benefits such as family allowances.

Table 22

TAXES AS A PERCENTAGE OF G.N.P. 1970

Social taxes	14·5
Indirect taxes	15·3
Direct taxes	7·0
All taxes	36·8

Table 23

CAPITAL INVESTMENT 1946–8
(As percentage of G.N.P. 1938 prices)

1946	*1947*	*1948*
21·1	21·8	20·4

During the earlier plans, the main aim of the State was to maintain a satisfactory high level of capital investment,[1] thus enabling France to make good the stagnation of the interwar years and the destruction of the War. In order to achieve this aim, both inflation and several devaluations of the French currency were allowed. When the inflation got out of hand – and threatened to cause grave social unrest among the lower-paid workers – the State resorted to price freezes which tended to become fairly effective after the initial teething troubles had been experienced.

During most of the period until de Gaulle's return to power in 1958, the greatest emphasis was placed on monetary policy, the use of subsidies and price freezes – with additional recourse to increases in the minimum basic wage (the S.M.I.C.) – and social benefits whenever the living standards of lower income groups came under serious pressure.

The stage for massive inflation was already set very shortly after the end of hostilities. In both 1944 and 1945, major wage increases and increases in family allowances occurred. Although a monetary conversion did take place, it could in no way be compared with the currency reforms which were undertaken in Belgium and in Western Germany. There had been a large increase in money due to the war, and the straight conversion of this money supply without freezing any part of it made inflation

[1] In this context, the rôle of the *Fonds de Modernisation et d'Equipement* (F.D.E.S.) must be emphasised.

inevitable. The heavy wage increases and the increase in government expenditure – both on capital account and for military
purposes – made some form of freeze inevitable. Thus in 1947
the first wage and price freeze was introduced. This freeze was
made tolerable to some producers through the form of subsidies
particularly in the agricultural field. Subsequently, prior to the
very important prices policies of the 1960s, price freezes occurred
in 1950, 1952, 1953 (as a result of serious social unrest – when
price reductions were also accepted) and in 1954. Also in 1952
M. Pinay had introduced a sliding scale for prices and wages.

The budget deficits of the State (the *impasse*) became more
important and greater recourse was also made to the 'provision-
al' advances made by the *Banque de France*. To some observers
this use of monetary policy by the State might seem a little
unfair – particularly in view of the basically strict rules governing
private lending by banks. In 1948, these rules had become clear.
As in the United Kingdom, the use of bank rate was important.
More important (and of earlier origin) was the use of credit
ceilings and directives. There were also minimum reserve
requirements, *planchers*. The amount of rediscounting by the
Banque de France was limited, known as *plafonds*, anything
beyond the limits was available only at penal rates.[1]

It is essential to note that the use of credit policy was very
important in the first two plans when remarkable investment
levels were realised. Until the mid-1950s, credit was scarce and
the French State, acting through the *Conseil National de Crédit*
and the *Banque de France*, was able to channel the scarce
resources into the desired ends – particularly into capital
investment and the nationalised industries.[2]

Again, some observers have accused the French of misusing
monetary and banking policy contributing to cyclical disturb-
ances. Some examples included the policies adopted in the
period 1949/50, when a depression seemed imminent; then in

---

[1] For the best documented account of French banking until the recent reforms,
see J. G. S. Wilson, *French Banking Structure and Credit Policy* (G. Bell & Sons,
1957).
[2] Certain legal exceptions were also used for these purposes:
  (i) medium-term obligations of a specialised agency (e.g. the *Crédit National*)
      for equipment purposes.
  (ii) Treasury paper which was used to supply working capital to exporters
       was completely freed at a later date.

1951 in increasing the monetary supply by over 30% through government borrowing from the banking system. Again, it is important to remember that the reconstruction of the economy took precedence over general macro-economic policy.

The period 1952–4 is noted as being one of temporary stability. The period had all the signs of a minor recession as economic activity slowed down a little. But basically, the real reasons for this stability were the effective price freezes – which led to real gains in productivity.

Although the budgetary deficit was maintained during this time, it was decided that some expansion must occur during the ensuing eighteen months. Thus the Faure Plan of expansion was introduced. The first measures took the form of important wage increases for the lower-paid workers. There were increases in capital investment and consequently in productivity. The expansion of the period is well demonstrated by table 24 below
.

Table 24

INCREASES IN FRENCH CONSUMPTION

1953–7	%
Food	14·0
Clothing	18·5
Housing	35·0
Hygiene/Health	34·0
Transport/Television	31·5
Culture/Leisure	33·0
Total	23·0

Similarly, major increases in the national car park were noted.

1944	1953	1957
910,000	3,266,000	5,818,000

The period also produced the first balance of payments surplus (1955/6), and as a result the normally stringent French exchange restrictions were temporarily relaxed.

Unfortunately the dormant inflation was awakened. Bank rate had been low in 1954, it continued at a low level into 1955. Then in the following year, the Suez Crisis and the war in

Algeria intensified the newly-awakened inflation. For the first time, stringent monetary and fiscal controls – together with the use of the devaluation of the currency – were contemplated and used.

In 1956, hire-purchase restrictions were first introduced. As in Britain, their influence was found to be effective but short-term in character. In the following year as controls on trade were introduced,[1] restrictions were placed on the use of *planchers* and *plafonds*, bank rate was increased to the penal level of 5% and indirect taxes were increased by 32%. At the same time subsidies were cut, and in 1958 the *Conseil National de Crédit* introduced a *Limitation des Encours* for a duration of one year.

The efficacy of the more rigid economic weapons being used in the late 1950s was particularly evident in the field of monetary control where as just indicated a series of measures were being used simultaneously: an increase in the price of credit, increased liquidity reserves and credit ceilings.[2]

In a series of enquiries which were conducted by the I.N.S.E.E. during the period 1957–9,[3] with French industrialists, it was noted that in 1956, only between 16 and 19% of the industrialists taking part in the survey complained about lack of finance for their businesses. During the course of 1957, this number rose to 24% and then to 44%. By the summer of 1958, a slight fall was noted (the figure being 43%), but by the end of that year, 46% of the industrialists were having difficulty in finding finance for their business activities.

Much greater criticism has been levied by French industrialists regarding the V.A.T., which they complain leads to the removal of finances (which might have been used for capital investment) from business enterprises. The analytical criticism which business men level at this tax (which was created in 1954 and extended to all business enterprises in 1966) concerns mainly the *butoir*. The *butoir* is simply the payment of taxes, for example, on raw materials, which may be higher than those levied on the finished product. This naturally penalises those firms engaged in initial production processes and those which

[1] 20% tax concessions to exporters. 20% tax on imports.

[2] This was particularly the case in 1957 and 1958.

[3] Note: *Etudes et Conjoncture*, June 1957, February and March 1958, February 1959.

use large quantities of raw materials. Further, where taxes are deductible at the later production stages, this is done after a delay of one month. This practice creates financial difficulties for some firms. Since, also, France does not admit to the reimbursement of taxes, some business enterprises see in this principle an additional source of any financial difficulties they may have.

This criticism must of course be somewhat neutralised by the fact that during the period 1956–9, French firms were allowed to write-off their equipment more swiftly than had hitherto been the case.

SPECIAL NOTE ON MONETARY AND FISCAL POLICY

During the period under review, one should not forget that the task of channelling the resources of the nation into the desired ends, via monetary policy, was made easier by the very nature of the monetary system.

First the stock exchange (the *Bourse*) was (and still is) very narrow. Then it has been normal (when not actually hoarding cash or gold at home!) for Frenchmen to place their money in banks rather than with insurance companies. Also building societies are of very recent origin in France. Thus, apart from any State subsidies, French businessmen were thrown into the arms of the banks. Until 1966 there was a strict division between the deposit banks (which could not make medium – and long-term loans, arrange new issues nor participate in business companies), the *banques d'affaires* and the specialised credit instutues such as the

> *Crédit Agricole*
> the *Crédit Populaire*
> the *Caisse des Dépôts et Consignations*[1]
and the *Crédit National*[2]

To this list should be added the *Crédit Foncier*, which is a

---

[1] This organisation holds all the funds accumulated in the local savings banks, the pension funds of nationalised industries and unspent tax revenue. The rôle of this institute is to transform short-term resources into medium-term credits for industry and to underwrite bond issues on the capital market.

[2] This institute supervises medium-term credit and will, in certain situations, guarantee medium-term loans to clients of commercial banks.

form of state building society created at the beginning of the last century, which grants mortgages to clients who are able to obtain an initial loan – constituting the deposit (normally about 20% of the purchase price) for the mortgage.

Since the French businessmen were and still are, to a large degree, forced to rely on bank credit, the fact that all applications for medium-term credit for business and industry were examined by the *Conseil National de Crédit*, the *Banque de France* and the *Commissariat du Plan*, is adequate indication of the State control over credit. The exception to this control appeared in 1970 when it was found that some companies were escaping national monetary control by lending to each other. This led to the changes in monetary controls which are discussed at the end of this book.

Monetary Terms

1. *Coefficient de Trésorerie:* Liquidity ratio. The National Credit Council required banks to maintain a minimum proportion of their reserves in the form of treasury bills varying between 20% and 35% by law (1960–70).

2. *Plafonds:* The maximum level of rediscounting done daily by the *Banque de France* at favourable rates.

3. *Planchers:* The minimum reserve in treasury bills.

4. *Pénalités:* Special deposits. In France, no interest is paid on these deposits.

5. *Limitation des Encours:* Credit ceilings, also called (the policy): *encadrement de crédit.*

Fiscal Policy

It has been noted that France relies heavily on indirect taxes and social security taxes in the use of fiscal policy. At the moment (1971) the ratio is about as follows:

	%
Indirect taxes	66
Direct taxes	34
	100

As we shall see in the final chapter, plans are now being made to change this ratio.

Of particular help to exporters was the introduction of the value added tax in 1954, and its subsequent generalisation in 1966. At the present time, there are four rates for this tax, 7·5%, 17·60%, 23% and 33·33%.[1] The lowest rate is applied to essentials such as food and books, the highest rate to such luxuries as sports cars. Although some British observers consider that the introduction of the *Carte d'Exportateur*,[2] in 1957, to help export industries, has achieved its aims, many French observers tend to emphasise more strongly the importance to exporters of the rebate they receive through the use of the value added tax.

As in most countries, there are a number of tax incentives to industrialists, intending to set up or to expand plant in the regions away from the capital. Special zones, with varying incentives, were created in 1964. In the Paris region, on top of the normal social security taxes which can account for up to 40% of the wages bill, there is a special tax on office workers. There also exists a transport tax on workers which is reimbursed to workers for use in travelling to their place of work.

In 1966, the French Government in an attempt to increase private investment in industry, introduced the now somewhat notorious *Avoir Fiscal*. This represents a substantial reimbursement on distributed dividends. Contrary to the experience of Western Germany (which served as the model for this exercise), there is no evidence which suggests that this concession has led to any increase in private investment in industry.

Few studies have been made concerning the precise impact of the use of fiscal policy in France.[3] It is known however that prior to 1958, changes in spending by the State in the public sector could have an impact equivalent to a change of up to 5% in the G.N.P. This is perfectly understandable when one considers the increase in indirect taxes by 32% in 1958. Since that date, greater emphasis has been placed on the use of monetary policy and the use of prices and incomes policies. As a result of this

[1] The full social implications of the use of this tax are examined at the end of this chapter.

[2] This is applied to firms with a minimum turnover of 375,000 francs, of which over 20% is exported.

[3] For the only complete study of the use of taxes in anti-cyclical policy in France, see Y. Fréville, *'L'Imposition des revenus des ménages et de la conjoncture'* in *Statistiques et Etudes Financières* (April 1968).

change in policy, budgetary changes have since accounted for a maximum change of 2·9% in the G.N.P. This is still very large by British standards.

THE FRENCH SYSTEM OF NATIONAL PLANNING

The recognition by the French State that it could influence capital investment[1] as a producer, buyer and financier is referred to again in the next section. The fact that government contracts, tax and other financial concessions were used by the French State to influence businessmen in their decisions has been described by many authors.[2] The field of planning which has never been properly analysed is that concerning the changes in the qualitative attitude of French businessmen to business activities through their association with the planning process. In the next few pages, the author proposes to attempt to analyse the changes in the attitudes of French businessmen to economics and management. But first, a few observations concerning the French State and its use of planning would be useful.

When the hostilities ceased, it is a well-known fact that not only had the damage of war to be repaired, but the gap of the 1920s and the 1930s had also to be made good. The State was in control of both credit and the import of raw materials. Further, apart from the fact that over 50% of capital investment could be influenced by State decisions, the State, whenever it took a participation in a company, always used its influence most categorically. This attitude contrasts strongly with that of the British Government, which, for example, when it had a 51·5% holding in B.P., did not use its powers particularly strongly – as against the French State's minority holding in the *Compagnie Française des Pétroles*, which was used most energetically.

It should not be forgotten also that when the French planning

---

[1] In the year 1959, French Government direct investment was responsible for 50·9% of total capital investment and was made up as follows: productive investment: 31·5%, infrastructure: 6·2%, housing: 13·2%.
[2] Especially by B. Cazes, *La Planification en France et le IVe Plan* (Editions de L'Epargne, 1962); P. Massé, *Le Plan ou L'Anti-hasard* (N.R.F., 1965); P. Bauchet, *L'Expérience française de planification* (du Seuil).

process was created at the beginning of 1946, it was done in the euphoria of a mass of social reforms and acts of nationalisation, carried out by de Gaulle's coalition government. Also the pragmatic attitude of the State was notable in normally suggesting a number of possible growth targets, and, having decided upon one, then proceeding together with business, civil service and social partners, to devise the means of attaining the goal. Fundamentally, the philosophy was that a target must be set – otherwise why have any planning at all?

Initially, when the planning apparatus was set up, the businessmen were not particularly enthusiastic about the operation. When in 1963 however, through the stabilisation plan, the existing planning system was in effect dropped, the businessmen lobbied the government for the maintenance of the Plan. The fall in business activity, as shown in the next section, amply demonstrates the degree to which businessmen had been accustomed to the planning process.

Businessmen have been closely associated with the Plan on both the forecasting side and regarding the targets or objectives of the Plan and their realisation. It is most important that the full implications of this fact be understood. Apart from the First Plan, when France did not have the statistical services which she now has, the market research for each branch of commercial and industrial activity has been both detailed and thorough. The association of businessmen with this medium-term forecasting and market research has meant that firms and industries have been forced to examine all possible markets for their products, which, in turn, has reduced excessive over-production. Equally, the possibility (there have obviously been cases of this happening) of business enterprises blackmailing the State into the granting of contracts and financial concessions for the creation of over-production, has been reduced.

In the realisation of the targets, the attitude of the State towards businessmen has been somewhat different. Basically, the question asked by the State is, 'what concessions and aid will be necessary to achieve our objectives?' Having made the relevant decisions, and having started the Plan off on its path, the possibility of bottlenecks or *Goulots d'Etranglement* arising cannot be avoided. It is here, perhaps, where the French planning process has been most successful. It has normally

devised short- and medium-term measures which have successfully removed such bottlenecks.

The actual number of businessmen associated directly with
the preparation of any one plan is limited. The late Professor
Houssiaux maintained further that only about fifty large French
firms centred their management decisions round the plan. In
contrast with this conclusion, studies conducted by both the
I.N.S.E.A.D. and the I.N.S.E.E. led to very different results.
The results of the 1967 Study conducted by the I.N.S.E.E. with
a sample of 2000 firms are given below:

Table 25

I.N.S.E.E. STUDY 1967: FRENCH FIRMS

	Number of employees per firm				
Percentage of firms having:	*10–99*	*100–499*	*500–999*	*1000–4999*	*5000+*
a system of management control	14	26	39	57	78
an economic research unit	6	9	16	31	79

This study would seem to confirm the observations made by
a number of economists that the top French firms which are
responsible for so large a percentage of the total national
turnover must be very good indeed.[1]

It would also be wrong to ignore the fact that tremendous publicity is given to planning in France in the press and on radio and
television. It is impossible that this information and the atmosphere of expansion which it generates is ignored by other firms.

The study carried out by the I.N.S.E.A.D. indicated that
many firms do indeed base their investment decisions on the
National Plan. The Plan helped most firms to judge the degree
of scope for their products at national level. In turn, new
investments would be made with regard to the possible ability
of existing productive capacity to meet an increase in demand

[1] The journal *Entreprise*, in an article '*Le Bilan des Bilans*' (8 March 1971),
indicated that 63·9 % of all French firms (responsible for 5·3 % of total national
business) had an annual turnover of less than 1 million francs, 0·4 % had a
turnover of more than 100 million francs (responsible for 36·5 % of business)
and 10·3 % had a turnover of between 5 and 100 million francs.

as a result of the realisation of and the forecasts made by the National Plan.

However, we should note that even in its heyday, the system of planning in France has not been free of criticism. Although the global targets have normally been met, they have not always been met in the individual branches of the economy. It has, as in other countries, been difficult to plan agriculture and forecast the balance of payments.[1] Planning has not always avoided a wastage of resources – as the proliferation of petrol stations in the country shows. Equally, failing industries have been supported in many cases, rather than seeking the implantation of new industries and the 're-cycling' of workers in the dying ones.

Socially, the planning system has frequently been bitterly criticised. The representation of the trade unions has always been weak. The earlier plans, in their obsession with heavy industry and later, with the consumption industries, were criticised for their weaker emphasis on the social infrastructure of the country. Until the Fifth and Sixth Plans, the question of income redistribution was ignored.

Nevertheless, until 1963, the French planning system did contribute to the creation of an atmosphere of expansion and confidence, which is only now being recreated. Lastly, without such a system, such notable projects as the twenty-year plan for the modernisation and electrification of the railway system would never have been realised.

FISCAL, MONETARY AND PRICES AND INCOMES POLICIES 1958–72

The unexpected return to power of General de Gaulle in 1958 coincided with France's entry into the European Economic Community. It was questioned whether de Gaulle would accept his country's membership of this organisation. Sensing that France's political influence might increase through membership of the Community, it was decided that she should not leave the new organisation.

With or without a change in the attitude of the new government regarding France's national aims in the economic sphere,

[1] Some sectors, such as defence, have not even been covered by the Plan.

some change in economic policy would have been necessary in view of her membership of the European Economic Community. Henceforth, it would be extremely difficult for France to maintain a high level of capital investment – using inflation, devaluations of the currency and important loans from abroad as the vehicle for this investment. Furthermore, with the accelerated reduction of tariff barriers, French firms, traditionally protected by high tariffs, would be increasingly exposed to the competition of her European neighbours. In many ways, the high level of capital investment that had been achieved prior to France's membership of the Common Market, increased her competitive position in the Community.

Apart from accepting France's membership of the European Economic Community, de Gaulle also desired to make the French franc a 'hard' currency, and eventually to make Paris the capital market of the Common Market. In his initial aim, he was both advised and helped by Pinay and Rueff. In the early attempts to cut down internal demand and inflation, a wide series of measures was adopted.

As already mentioned, an increase in indirect taxes of 32% had already been agreed upon in the previous year, to take effect in 1958. This fiscal decision was maintained. In a much more moderate manner, there were also slight increases in direct taxation, both personal and business. But the difficulty of collection of these taxes and the time lag involved meant that the effects on the economy were minimal.

Certain subsidies which had been created in 1956 (such as a subsidy to the railways) were abolished, and the nationalised industries were asked to balance their budgets. As far as the railways were concerned, the dropping of the subsidy had an inflationary influence since they increased fares by 20%. Again, in the case of the French railways, we should not forget that their attempts to remain solvent have always been aggravated by the important reductions they give to large families (*Familles Nombreuses*), invalids, civil servants and other members of the nation who may describe themselves as 'defavourised'.

One of the main aims put forward by Pinay and Rueff even before their Report, *Pour le redressement de la situation économique*, published in December, was the return of confidence to the currency and in the economy in general. To this end, they persuaded the government to decree a fiscal amnesty for French-owned capital abroad. This did result in a return of some of the capital formerly held outside the country. The return of this capital might have rendered difficult the management of inflation had the famous tax-free State Loan, the *Emprunt-Pinay* not been floated.

Acting upon the recommendations of the Pinay-Rueff Report, the French franc, after having been devalued by 17·5% in December 1958, was then made convertible.

It is highly probable that a combination of circumstances contributed to France's return to a balance of payments surplus in the following year, 1959. Without doubt, the splendidly high level of capital investment, maintained almost continuously since 1946, gave France a reserve of modern productive capacity. (See Table 26 below.) A recent book, written by three Frenchmen,[1] stresses the importance of their country's obsession

Table 26

CAPITAL INVESTMENT 1949–69
(As a percentage of G.N.P.)

	1949	*1952*	*1957–60*	*1966*	*1969*
Total investment	19·7	17·8	21·2	24·1	25·0
Productive investment	14·6	11·7	13·4	14·1	15·0

with renewing and rebuilding the national productive capacity – sometimes at costs which could not have been contemplated by a country like the United Kingdom, concerned with managing the pound sterling as a reserve currency, concerned with its special relations with both the Commonwealth and the United States of America, and maintaining a diplomatic and military presence internationally – quite out of keeping with her resources.

The national planning process, inaugurated in 1946, alongside the wave of nationalisations of the base sectors of the economy carried out by the first de Gaulle government, was responsible for the renewal of the public infrastructure (continuing until the

[1] J. Carre, P. Dubois, E. Malinvaud, *La Croissance française: un essai d'analyse économique causale d'après-guerre* (du Seuil, 1972).

present moment in the case of the State railway system). It was also responsible, until the middle 1950s, for the devotion of important resources to heavy industry. But normally (and hence the disappointment caused by the stabilisation plan of 1963–5 inclusive) the national plans created a climate of optimism for businessmen – particularly those who relied on the State for

Table 27

NATIONAL PLANS: FORECASTS AND RESULTS

	II Plan (1952–7)		III Plan (1957–61)		IV Plan (1959–65)		V Plan (1965–70)	
	Forecast	*Result*	*Forecast*	*Result*	*Forecast*	*Result*	*Forecast*	*Result*
P.I.B.*	124	130	120	116	138	140	132	133

* *Produit Intérieur Brut.*

contracts.[1] This optimum was maintained when the emphasis moved from the public sector to the private industrial manufacturing sector.

Thus, as France joined the European Economic Community, she had all the necessary productive capacity at her disposal – together with a rising birthrate – only the continuous inflation had caused the prices of France's products to move out of line with those of her competitors. The 1958 devaluation brought her prices into line with those of her Common Market partners as the first tariffs were removed in 1959. The confidence in the franc caused by the fiscal amnesty and the return to convertibility in the previous year, encouraged the movement of funds into France. Later, at an industrial structural level, the State encouraged mergers in an attempt to form French companies. of an international size, able to compete with foreign companies. In this field, it is notable that the French State has always used

[1] As already mentioned, in the immediate postwar years, the State had observed that it could influence the direction and level of capital investment through its three-fold rôle as a producer (in the nationalised industries), as a buyer (for example, of rolling stock for the State railways) and as a financier. As a financier, not only did the State control credit, but could also make loans on advantageous terms and could offer many fiscal concessions to business men. Since 1956, the famous 'Lois-Programme' has ensured that capital investment is planned on a five-year basis and forms the base of each budget. In France fiscal policy is concerned with the allocation of resources, for example, to capital investment, rather than with the collection of revenue.

its powers of intervention with vigour. When in 1963 it was decided that the *Compagnie Française Des Pétroles* should have half of the French market, the foreign petrol companies were simply ordered to give up part of their market to the French company! By 1965 the French company controlled half of the market.

It is important to note that in 1959, when the emphasis was placed on a more careful and balanced management of the economy, at no time was there any intention of reducing the level of capital investment – even in the public sector. Instead, perhaps surprisingly, military expenditure was cut and reductions were made in the servicing of public sector investment. Then, in May, in an attempt to help industry, accelerated depreciation allowances were introduced for certain industrial investments. Encouragement was also given to foreign investment in France.

In the field of planning the next years are important for the country. In 1960, an intermediate plan had to be introduced to prolong the life of the Third Plan which started in 1957. The year 1960 is however particularly important since M. Pinay leaves the Ministry of Finance and is replaced by M. Baumgartner. M. Giscard d'Estaing is Secretary of the Budget; controlling these ministers is M. Debré, the Prime Minister. It is at this moment that the first important signs of economic philosophical conflict become apparent between Debré and Giscard d'Estaing, a conflict which becomes acute as the Fourth Plan (1962–5) is finalised in the second half of 1961. Debré, a Jacobin, is a faithful servant of the State and of the Plan, and he particularly wishes to preserve the planning system. At the same time he harasses the employers' confederation (C.N.P.F.) to keep down wages and to move their investments into the regions. His concern with the level of wages is perfectly reasonable since there had been increases throughout the public sector and increases in the family allowances in 1960. Also there had been a partial return to the price index system and it had been agreed that 80 % of social security costs would be reimbursed to patients.

Giscard d'Estaing, in contrast with Debré, is a member of the *Haute Bourgeoisie*, a liberal economist and opposed to planning. It is possible that some of his attitudes have now changed, but in 1961, he was, in the field of economics, very different from Debré.

The first signs of the renewed inflation which was to become particularly disquieting in 1962 were already beginning in 1961 when the price of meat shot upwards. Here, in the field of agriculture, improvements in the correct type of mechanisation were slow to materialise and too much emphasis had been placed on wheat production. The necessary structural changes were taking longer to materialise than had been anticipated.

However, at the beginning of 1962, Giscard d'Estaing became Finance Minister and a few months later, Debré was replaced by Pompidou as Prime Minister. Thus the stage was set for a change in national economic management, which, surprisingly, took a eight full months to materialise. Throughout most of the year, attempts were made to fulfil de Gaulle's philosophy of a 'gaullist socialism'. One of the main planks in this philosophy was worker participation in industry, as symbolised by the Amendement Vallon. This legislation was only enacted at a later date (in 1965).

In 1963 there were three increases in family allowances and also an increase in the minimum national wage (the S.M.I.C.) far in excess of price increases. At the end of 1961, the Renault car company had awarded a fourth week's annual paid holiday to their employees. Since improvements in pay and working conditions in this State enterprise tend to be adopted in other sectors of the economy, it was not surprising when three quarters of a million metal workers in the Paris region also received the fourth week's paid holiday in 1962.

On the military side, extra credits were voted for the *Force de Frappe*, thus helping to maintain a heavy budget deficit.

But the real cause for alarm in 1962 was the huge influx of refugees from Algeria following the conclusion of the peace at Evian. Nothing on this scale had been anticipated. In the space of eighteen months, the population of France increased by 7%! Many of these people brought money with them which swelled the credit-creating base of the country. And then, on arrival in France, the State gave them finance. Much of the finance went into the purchase of small businesses, much went into speculation in luxury apartment construction, in turn removing resources from other more social forms of building.

In the year 1962, prices increased by 4·8%, wages by 8·6% and productivity by 6·8%. Governmental alarm first manifested itself through credit restrictions, credit having increased by 18% in the one year! First, the maximum increase in credit for the coming year was limited to 12%. Then the obligatory liquidity ratio (*Coefficients de Trésorerie*) was increased from 32% to 35%, later to be raised to 36%.

But the real weapon which is to be used in the attempt to control prices is the famous stabilisation plan which was to last until the end of 1965. Although, as we shall see, prices did fall, a certain cost was involved in realising this achievement. The slow-down in economic activity meant the real end of French planning as we had known it since 1946. The stabilisation plan shook the confidence of French businessmen with the result that capital investment fell in the years 1964 and 1965. Even now it is doubtful whether the lost confidence has been regained. At this point the stabilisation plan and its results deserve a closer examination.

The Stabilisation Plan 1962–5

Basically, this plan aimed at reducing the expansion which had originally been forecast in the Fourth Plan. It also aimed at controlling prices and wages.

Prices were restricted to their level as of 31 August 1962. Planned price increases were forbidden by law and wages were frozen.

It was intended to reduce and possibly remove the budget deficit. The means used to this end were the premature release of young men from national service, the introduction of controls over loans for construction and the floating of a State loan. As already mentioned, monetary controls were immediately stiffened; the liquidity ratio was raised to 36%, and there was an increase in the bank rate. The liquidity reserve ratio is varied over the next two years and the bank credit restrictions do not end until the summer of 1965.

Unfortunately, the slow-down in prices[1] and the wage freeze

---

[1] It is interesting to note the use of the *Contrats de Stabilité* which were concluded at this time. These were agreements made with the Minister of Finance, allowing firms to increase certain prices if they made equivalent reductions elsewhere.

resulted in a fall in capital investment and the diminished ability of French business and industry to finance itself. Thus a period of encouragement and expansion is vitally necessary – in

Table 27A

PRICE INCREASES 1963–6

1963	1964	1965	1966
+ 5·0 %	+ 3·1 %	+ 2·8 %	+ 2·8 %

January 1966, Giscard d'Estaing is replaced by Debré at the Ministry of Finance and attempts are made to expand the economy.

The 'Relance Economique' 1966–8

The decision to stimulate the economy came as the Fifth Plan was already being executed and as the publication of the *Rapport Montjoie* on French business firms was being prepared.

Table 28

RAPPORT MONTJOIE

		Profits of French Firms		
		1955	1960	1965–6–7
		% 4·4	% 4·0	% 3·5

Self-Financing (as a percentage of total financing) of French Firms

1959	1960	1961	1962	1963	1964	1965	1966	1967
83	76	66	66	62	57	71	65	65

Although this report was not published until 1967, its findings were already known to the government and gave a clear but grave picture of the results of the stagnation in the economy.

Thus there were two main aims in the new economic policy. Firstly, the greatest encouragement would be given to the channelling of savings to finance capital investment. As an initial major stimulus, the government planned a 40% increase in public investment for 1966 over the level of the previous year. Similarly, the newly-introduced *Avoir Fiscal* was intended to encourage the re-investment of distributed profits. Then the specialised banks were given much greater freedom in their lending policies.[1]

Secondly the State wished to encourage mergers in order to produce French companies of international size. Thus, in 1966, there were mergers between Sud and Nord Aviation and between Dassault and Breguet. In the automobile industry, a working agreement was reached between the State concern Renault, and the private firm, Peugeot. Unfortunately, instead of restricting the shipbuilding industry, the State gave it an exceptional grant of 130 million francs.

The measures introduced in 1966 failed to produce any significant results in the following year and the underused capacity manifested itself in the form of the beginnings of unemployment among the flood of young people entering the labour market early in 1968. Here, it is worth noting the evolution of the population and its structure since 1958. The total population had increased by 12%, the young population by 40%.

Table 29

TOTAL POPULATION: YOUNG PERSONS 1958–67

In millions	*Total*	
1958	44·5	5·7
1967	50·0	8·0

Almost intuitively anticipating the 'May Events' of 1968, the government brought on stream additional investments – particularly for council housing (due to the speculation in luxury construction in the mid 1960s), there was an increase in family allowances of 4·5% (a second one of 4·5% took place in August), the first of three increases in pensions was made, accompanied by a cut in direct taxes.

As most observers know, following the 'May Events', two

---

[1] These measures are examined at the end of this chapter.

major wage agreements were made, one for industrial workers –
the '*Accords de Grenelle*' – and one for agricultural workers –
the '*Accords de Varenne.*' Apart from the increases in wages in
the industries listed below, the national minimum wage for
industrial workers (the S.M.I.G.) was increased by between
35 and 38%, and the equivalent for the agricultural workers
(the S.M.A.G.) by between 56 and 59%.

Table 30

THE 'ACCORDS DE GRENELLE' 1968
Wage Increases by Industry (percentages)

State Industries
15·0 – 15·4

Local Administration
19·2

Private Industry

Clothing	15·6	Petrol	10·0
Leather	14·5	Metal	10·5
Textiles	13·6	Glass	10·6

Consequences of the 1968 Agreements

The consequences of these agreements indicate quite clearly the
amount of unused capacity existing in the French economy –
largely as a result of the stabilisation measures of 1963–5 – a
degree of slack that had not yet been taken up in 1967. The
efficacy of the 1968 measures is amply demonstrated by the
increase in productivity of 7·8% accompanied by a price rise of
only 4·5%. However, the monetary supply increased by 18·5%,
and therefore constituted a potential explosive force for the
future. Also, one should not forget that one of the main national
economic aims of gaullist policy was the maintenance of the
franc as a 'hard' currency. Together with this aim was the desire
to make Paris the capital market of the European Economic
Community. Already in 1967, many exchange controls had been
removed, and Paris was well on the way to becoming the
Community's short-term supplier of capital.[1] This achievement
perished on the May barricades in 1968. As a result of the

[1] See P. Coffey and J. R. Presley, 'London and the Development of a European
Capital Market', in *The Bankers' Magazine* (June 1971).

accompanying speculation against the franc, France was reluctantly forced to re-impose exchange controls. Since, as his speech later in the year indicated, de Gaulle had no intention of devaluing the franc, some of the newly-created demand had to be syphoned off – if only in a window-dressing fashion reminiscent of similar actions taken in favour of the pound sterling. In the monetary field, the measures took the form of increases in bank rate to 6% and the imposition of credit ceilings. In the fiscal field, there were temporary increases of between 10 and 22% in the upper levels of direct taxation (which were not finally dropped until 1971) – though their imposition and effect were not immediate. Of more immediate consequence were the increases in car taxes and some other V.A.T. levels. Lastly, the budget deficit was cut and price controls were re-introduced.

The increase in productivity in 1968 had certainly used up much of the slack in the French economy. However the continued influx of young workers on to the labour market did continue and would have provided an additional reserve of productivity had not the diverse aims of the State caused difficulties in the national economic management. To many outside observers, the franc was over-valued (though this belief may be questioned) and this increased the speculation against the currency. It was also impossible for the French economy to produce all the extra output needed to meet the demands caused by the previous year's great wage increases. Thus, when everyone was away on holiday, the franc was devalued in August 1969 in a swift and successful operation.[1] The devaluation was accompanied by an austerity programme, aimed at influencing one of the biggest generators of income, the public investment programmes. One-sixth of public investment was frozen and placed in a special fund, the *Fonds d'Action Conjoncturelle*.

The austerity programme was continued in 1970 when a further 10% of public investment programmes were frozen and the loans made by the F.D.E.S. were reduced by a third; the rate of interest on the remaining two-thirds was increased. These actions led to the balancing of the budget.

Together with this effective programme of austerity in the

[1] The success was heightened by the German revaluation which led to a further increase in France's international competitive position.

public investment field, a most rigid monetary policy was adopted. In March 1970, banks which did not respect the credit ceilings were forced to place a 100% equivalent of the loans given above the ceiling with *Banque de France* – on these deposits they received no interest payments. Similarly the French bank rate was raised to the unheard-of level of 8 %! This rise in the bank rate was to have the same inconvenience as has been experienced by Britain and other countries practising the same policy. France wished to dampen down expansion at home but found that the high bank rate encouraged speculators to move money into France – thus enlarging the credit-creating base of the country and creating a potential source of inflation. Even though the bank rate was reduced in the summer of 1970 and again in 1971, it neither encouraged economic activity at home, nor did it discourage to any significant degree the inflow of funds from abroad. Further, the still unusually high bank rate encouraged much saving by individuals in France throughout 1971. The resultant extraordinary increase in bank liquidity (the money supply increased by 17·4% over the 1970 level) was not taken up by borrowers and thus had a dampening effect on the economy, further accentuating the already un-acceptably high unemployment levels among young people.

In the summer and autumn of 1970, in an attempt to combat unemployment, the measures of the previous eighteen months were reversed, 1·1 billion francs were de-frozen from the *Fonds d'Action Conjoncturelle* and channelled into road, housing and school construction. Also, hire purchase regulations were eased, the tax on cars reduced from 33·3 to 23·4%, and the extra supplementary income tax was dropped (this last measure did not become effective until 1971).

The continued high unemployment levels early in 1971 led to an intensification of the measures just mentioned and the introduction of more novel measures (examined more closely in the next and final section). The continued rise in prices led to the conclusion of a *Contrat Anti-Hausse* with the employers in September. Lastly, the inefficiency of the monetary policy caused the government to introduce changes, late in the year, which brought French banking practices more into line with those of other countries.

1971 was also the year of the major international monetary

crisis when the French introduced two markets for the franc, one the commercial franc for current commercial trading purposes, and the financial franc for speculative or investment purposes. In the former case, fixed exchange rates were observed, in the latter case, they would float.

France had already taken many steps to discourage the inflow of funds from abroad; she had always forbidden her businessmen to borrow short-term from the euro-dollar market, non-residents were forbidden to open bank accounts in the country, interest payments were not paid on existing non-resident bank deposits, and, as always, non-residents could not purchase French Treasury paper.

In an attempt to encourage the outflow of funds, necessitated by the balance of payments surplus, France made easier the sale of non-French securities in the country and the purchasing of such securities by French nationals. Also the amounts of money which Frenchmen could transfer abroad or take out of the country were substantially increased. All these measures contrast strongly with French policies in the previous decade.

Special Note on the French Prices and Incomes Policies

As we have already seen, the first attempt at a prices and incomes policy, 1963–5, was a complete success. It is worth looking at this experiment in a little more detail since the policy was more complete than is normally imagined by outside observers. When the prices policy was first introduced in September 1963, it was applied solely to the 'productive' industries which included the food and agricultural sectors, but excluded the agricultural 'non-transformation' industries, for example, butter. The price level taken was 31 August. The only exceptions made to this rule could be made on the express authority of the Ministry of Finance and Economic Affairs. Then, on 20 November, certain service industries (for example, woodwork firms) were included in the ban together with over twenty purely service industries (for example, publicity and schools giving driving lessons). In these cases, some price levels were those as on 31 August, in others, those of 31 October.

Again, as already noted, a certain flexibility was introduced early in 1965 through the use of the *Contrats de Stabilité*. However these agreements could only be made where there were certain legitimate reasons for price increases such as an increase in the price of raw materials. In this manner over twenty such agreements were made.

In March 1966, as the price freeze proper ended, it was increasingly felt that something should replace the experience of the previous two years (it is possible that this continuity is the real reason for the relative French success in this field – among other reasons). The new measures adopted became known as *Contrats de Programme* and were intended to stop the infernal stop-go cycle of inflation and price freezes. The new agreement is novel in that it took the form of an agreement made with the State both by employers and trade unions (on a firm or industry basis, or both). The agreement covers wages, prices and productivity and is given a quality of continuity by the annual (sometimes more than once a year) meetings between the Treasury and the heads of enterprises and their aides. Gradually most of the French industry has signed such agreements with the State.

At this point, the burning question which must be answered is, just how effective has this policy been, and what weapons can the State use against recalcitrant firms and industries? Perhaps the second question is easier to answer. The State, in cases of exorbitant price increases, has withdrawn from the culprits the concessions which they were receiving through the National Plan.

The first question is best answered by the following table:

Table 31

PRICE RISES 1966–70 (ON A PERCENTAGE BASIS)
(Over previous year)

1966	1967	1968	1969	1970
2·9	2·8	4·8	7·9	5·7

If the results have not been as handsome as one might have expected, we should not forget the role of the important wage increases to which the State was a party in 1968, the inflow of funds into France in 1970 and 1971, together with the subsequent good performance on the commercial account of the balance of payments which was possibly an importer of inflation.

The State nevertheless believes that the *Contrats de Programme* are important since the first ones were extended beyond the end of 1970, first until the end of 1971 and then until 10 March 1972.[1]

The main period of these agreements covers the 1968 episode when one must speak less of an agreement and more of an imposed freeze. Thus, in the second half of 1968, price increases were limited to 3%. This freeze was made more categorical in November when those industrialists who did not lower their prices equivalent to the exceptional removal of labour taxes (removed to help exports) would not be able to participate in the agreements, and the prices of their products would be frozen by law! The following year, after the franc had been devalued, all prices were frozen until 15 September at the level of 8 August. Again, the only exceptions to the rule were where the price of raw materials had increased. When the new freeze finished on 10 September, those businessmen who wished to increase the prices of their products were forced to first inform the Treasury of the proposed price increases. If within the space of a month the Treasury had made no objection to the proposals, the increases could go ahead. Again fundamental exceptions were made where the costs of raw materials had risen – but only where they constituted at least 30% of the total costs of the final product. In the following year, in February, this was reduced to 15%.

This new formula was gradually dropped as from this date. The rise in prices in the following year compelled the government to seek yet a new formula, the *Contrats Anti-Hausse*. In this case, the equivalent of the British C.B.I. – in France *le Patronat Français* – was asked to accept a limitation (with some exceptions) of 1·5% for price increases over the period 15 September 1971–15 September 1972.[2]

In the future most French economists believe that we are likely to witness a return, for some time, to the *Contrats de Programme*. The extension of these agreements into 1973 would seem to vindicate these forecasts.

THE SOCIAL EFFECTS OF THE FRENCH TAXATION SYSTEM

In reforming the V.A.T., the French State had hoped that the division of this tax into different levels, with a very low tax rate

---

[1] Subsequently extended into the Spring of 1973.
[2] These agreements were also extended into 1973.

being levied on essential goods, would in some way compensate for the less important rôle played by direct taxation in France. The direct tax levels (as shown in the following tables) are low, and are not as steeply progressive as in countries such as Britain and Western Germany. Since the professions and similar groups in France are very well-paid, the taxation system benefits them. Equally, the professional groups which have several children in their families are just as eligible for family allowances and tax concessions as are more modest wage-earners. Thus these benefits are not the vehicle of income redistribution, but rather incentives to an increased birth-rate. It is therefore understandable that the French State should reform the V.A.T. in the manner in which it did. (See Tables 32, 33 and 34.)

Table 32

DIRECT TAXATION ACCORDING TO INCOME GROUPS

	Weight of taxes on incomes in 1965[1]	
	In relation to the average income set out in the National Account[2]	*In relation to the primary average income*[3]
	%	%
Senior executives and liberal professions	11·4	12·5
Heads of business and industry	11·4	9·2
Executives	6·0	6·6
Employers	4·9	5·1
Workers	3·7	3·8
Farmers	4·7	3·1
Agricultural workers	3·3	3·3
Non-salaried	7·4	6·9
Total	7·2	7·4

[1] Progressive direct tax, supplementary tax, road tax, stamp tax.

[2] The study made by Madame Euvrard in *Projet*, February 1972, p. 185.

[3] *Economie et Statistique*, number 20.

Recently, a number of studies has been conducted and their results question the fairness of the V.A.T. as it affects different social groups. The one point (although the precise percentage does vary in each case) which these studies have in common is

Table 33

POPULATION AND INCOMES
(Percentage of total in 1969)

	Proportion of population	Proportion of Incomes
Low and moderately paid employees (80 % of total)	62	38
Upper salary levels (20 % of total)	15	29
Non-salaried	23	33

Source: *Responsables*, number 34, 1972.

Table 34

THE WEIGHT OF PAID TAXES ON WAGE EARNERS (1968)

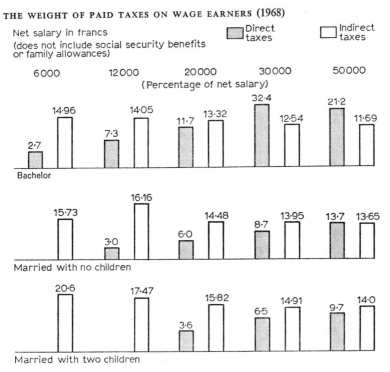

Net salary in francs
(does not include social security benefits or family allowances)

Direct taxes   Indirect taxes

6 000   12 000   20 000   30 000   50 000
(Percentage of net salary)

Bachelor: 2·7, 14·96, 7·3, 14·05, 11·7, 13·32, 32·4, 12·54, 21·2, 11·69

Married with no children: 15·73, 3·0, 16·16, 6·0, 14·48, 8·7, 13·95, 13·7, 13·65

Married with two children: 20·6, 17·47, 3·6, 15·82, 6·5, 14·91, 9·7, 14·0

Source: French Ministry of Finance, 1972.

that the weight of the V.A.T. is similar among the spending of French citizens, whatever their standard of living may be.

The first and most important study on the value added tax,

organised by the trade union, the C.F.D.T., and which was unfortunately not published,[1] indicated that the weight of the V.A.T. on the purchases of different social groups was as follows:

	%
Agricultural workers, industrial workers and office workers	15–16
Executives	16–17
Industrialists and members of the liberal professions	17

It was at first thought that this study was in itself unfair since the year of reference was 1965 which did not take account of the important changes in the S.M.I.C. and certain tax changes that have taken place during and since 1968.

The importance of this criticism and of the subject in itself led the Ministry of Finance to conduct a study with 1968 as the year of reference.[2] The results of this study showed that the variation in the weight of the indirect taxes on the purchases of different groups was quite small. In this study, the wage levels themselves were used as the reference, and resulted in the following spread:

	%
Monthly salary: 2,500 francs or less	12·7
Monthly salary: 2,500–5,000 francs	13·5
Monthly salary: 10,000 francs or above	14·4

Lastly, also in 1972, the *Commissariat Général du Plan* came to almost identical conclusions in a similar study. Here, indirect taxes accounted for between 12·6 and 15·1% of purchases according to different socio-professional groups. In the case of wage-earners, the range was 14·0–17·5%.

In all these studies, the conclusion that one can draw is that the number of items which are taxed at the lowest rate is not large, whilst the heavy taxes fall on an ever smaller number of articles. Thus most indirect taxes cover the vast central band of goods, purchased by members of all social groups. Equally, the professional and wealthier groups of the population receive further advantages in the form of the *Avoir Fiscal* on distributed profits, the absence of taxation on purchases of stocks and shares, the absence of taxes on government paper (the most

---

[1] Dassetto and Victor, *Une Atteinte à la progressivité de l'impôt: la T.V.A.* (1968).

[2] '*Statistiques et études financières*' in *Collection Orange*: No. 5 (1972), p. 39.

famous example here is the *Emprunt Pinay*) and through con-
tractual taxes which are only levied on bonds.

This situation in which a small proportion of the population
owns a large proportion of the national wealth (already
examined earlier in the section on 'Industry' in chapter 4), has
been further illuminated by a recent publication, specially consecrated to a study of the French taxation system,[1] which con-
cludes that even the educational and social services in the
country do not lead to the anticipated redistribution of income,
since (as in some other countries) it is often the more educated
persons who know what benefits are available and who proceed
to take advantage of them.

FRENCH BANKING REFORMS

The stabilisation Plan (1963–5) reduced the self-financing
possibilities of French businesses. Their difficulties were not
helped by the specialised nature of the French banks nor by the
narrowness of the *Bourse*. It was felt that reforms could most
easily be affected through changes in banking practices, and, in
1966, the distinction between the different types of banks was
abolished. This reform meant that banks could broaden their
activities and that merchant banks which had hitherto been
mainly confined to the Paris region could move out into the
provinces. But this also meant that, in order to broaden their
activities, some of the merchant banks would have to form links
with existing deposit banks,[2] and more recently, even with

---

[1] '*Réhabiliter l'impôt*' in *Projet* (February 1972).

[2] The following table (35) shows the most important French deposit banks
(in order of amounts of deposits) as at the end of June 1972. This table will have
probably changed at the time of publication as a new grouping was planned in
the summer of 1972 by the *Compagnie Financière de Paris et des Pays-Bas*
(normally known as the *Paribas*) and the *Banque Worms*. Into this regrouping
would be brought the *Banque de l'Union Parisienne* (B.U.P.) and the *Crédit du
Nord*. This new regrouping will be called the *Union Bancaire* and will then rival
the C.I.C. (*Crédit Industriel et Commercial*) in the table below. The latter was
substantially expanded when it passed under the control of the *Financière de
Suez* in the latter part of 1971.

It should be noted that, at the end of the last war, the then most important
deposit banks were nationalised. These were the *Crédit Lyonnais*, the *Société
Générale*, the *Banque Nationale pour le Commerce et l'Industrie*, and the *Comptoir
National d'Escompte de Paris*.

commercial enterprises not even remotely connected with banking.

In the former case, as soon as the banking reforms were being introduced, the *Paris-Bas* took a 3% holding in the *Crédit Industriel et Commercial*. A year later it started buying shares in the *Crédit du Nord*. However, as the *Paris-Bas* was taking over its holdings, a rival group, the *Compagnie Financière de Suez* and the *Banque de l'Union Parisienne*, had taken up a 7·0% share in the equity of the *Crédit Industriel et Commercial*. It needed the intervention of the Governor of the *Banque de France* to persuade the *Paris-Bas* and the *Suez-Union Parisienne* Group to place their C.I.C. equity holdings in a joint holding company.[1]

Table 35

LEADING DEPOSIT BANKS
(End June 1972)

	Amount of deposits in thousands of millions of francs
1. *B.N.P.*	64·15
2. *Crédit Lyonnais*	58·00
3. *Société Générale*	50·90
4. *Groupe C.I.C.*	23·00
5. *Groupe des Banques Populaires*	16·00
6. *Union Bancaire*	10·00
7. *Crédit Commercial de France*	8·40
8. *Banque de Paris et des Pays-Bas*	8·00
Not classified:	
Crédit Agricole	69·90
La Caisse des Dépôts et Consignations	142·00

This operation is the result of a very complicated set of events, dating back to 1971, and which really concern insurance operations rather than purely banking ones. It is indeed a very

[1] More recently, in June 1972, there has been a similar operation, this time involving the *L'Abeille S.A.*, the *S.A.*, and the *Compagnie Financière de Suez*. In this case, however, *La Paternelle* agreed to sell its holding amounting to 46% of the total capital of the *Banque d'Indochine* to the *Compagnie Financière de Suez*. This obviously gives great importance to the *Groupe Suez*.

good example of the diversification currently taking place in French banking. The series of events started with the creation of a holding company[1] in July 1971 by the *Compagnie Assurances Abeille et Paix* (C.A.A.P.) and the *Groupe Paternelle*. The participation of both groups in the management methods differed fundamentally. Thus, it was decided, in June 1972, to disband the operations, using the following methods. A society, made up of the *Groupe Suez* and the *Abeille*, received the shares in the Group formerly held by *Groupe Abeille-Paix*. The *Groupe Suez* and the *Abeille* returned the other half of the shares, plus profits, to the *Groupe Paternelle*. This operation having been completed, a new insurance group, the *Abeille et Paix*, was formed, 65·25% of the capital being held by *Abeille* and 34·75% by the *Groupe Suez*.

In 1968, at about the same time as building societies were being developed in France, the State was encouraging the banks to diversify their rôles still further, particularly by entering the house construction field. These increased activities of the banks, linked at times with relatively high interest rates, have led, particularly in 1971 and in 1972, to the accumulation of large deposits in the banking system which constitute a potentially explosive inflationary force in the economy.

It was to be anticipated that the national banking reforms, together with France's membership of the European Economic Community, would sooner or later lead to some form of European link-up between major French banks and their neighbours. In 1967 there was an important link-up between the *Banque Nationale de Paris* and other banks (including the British Barclays Bank) to form a European holding group known as the *Société Financière Européenne*. However, of much greater importance as a world potential challenger, was the link-up in 1970, between the *Crédit Lyonnais*, the *Banca di Roma* and the *Commerzbank*. This link-up provides a model of the type of co-operation which could materialise in the enlarged European Economic Community, but it is particular in being a link-up between two nationalised banks and an independent one. In general, the successful moves to both broaden and to diversify French banking practices would seem to indicate that France is gradually moving towards a department-store type of

[1] The A.G.P. – *Assurances de Groupe de Paris*.

range of banking services, similar to that already offered in Western Germany. Such an evolution already appears to be visible when one examines the current extraordinary increase in personal loans being made by French banks. This expansion had already begun late in 1968. Despite the *Encadrement de Crédit*, it expanded strongly during the first half of 1969, fell in the second half of that year, decreased further until the middle of 1970 when it started to rise once again. Expansion was marked throughout 1971 and at the moment (July 1972) it is expanding at the rate of 25% per annum. Currently, the borrowing price is about 12% which corresponds favourably with specialised lending agencies such as C.E.T.E.L.E.M., S.O.V.A.C. and D.I.A.C. This development, coinciding with the heavy spate of deposits and loans being made by building societies and similar specialised agencies, for house construction, makes the task of the national monetary authorities correspondingly more difficult.

Reference has already been made, in the section on agriculture, to the banking reforms of 1966, which allowed the important *Crédit Agricole* to diversify its activities. One change made by this reform was to make loans to individuals and organisations not specifically connected with agriculture. The next important step was to create subsidiary companies. The main subsidiary was the *Union d'Etudes et d'Investissements*, which has used its resources to finance individual enterprises. In 1971 this subsidiary, aware of the very important developments in the food processing sectors, created a further subsidiary, the *Unicrédit (L'Union pour le Développement Régional)*. As its name implies, this subsidiary is concerned mainly with regional development – but of a more specialised nature. It is mainly concerned with making loans to food processing and agricultural industries or similar activities in the regions which are likely to create jobs. As this subsidiary has not yet been recognised as a deposit bank, it is unable to own shares in the capital of companies.[1]

Although it is difficult to obtain any precise figures, the

[1] However, in July 1972, M. Giscard d'Estaing warned the *Crédit Agricole* against diversifying its activities too greatly. He pointed out that its vocation must be mainly agricultural and that its activities must be balanced between the profitable and the social (regional).

French deposit banks are now beginning (as is the case in Western Germany) to participate more actively in the ownership and management of business enterprises. It is too early, apart from the increased participation by banks in financing housing construction, to judge the degree to which these banking reforms have led to any substantial increase in the allocation of funds to industrial investment.

7 Current Changes in the Management of France's Economy

Introduction

During the past eighteen months, important changes have taken place in the management of France's national economy. These changes, which have passed almost unnoticed by British observers, affect all the major fields of economic management – and mark a substantial break with the past for France. It is the purpose of this section to examine these changes and to briefly suggest their possible implications.

But first, why should any changes have been necessary and what particular problems does France face at the present time? As in most countries, solutions which have been used effectively to remedy certain problems, have finished by producing their own antithesis. Thus, in the case of France, one of the immediate postwar problems was (apparently) the insufficient size of the French population, and consequently measures were adopted (for example, major increases in family allowances) which, it was hoped, would encourage an increase in the population (apart from immigration, which was mainly used to increase the work force). The French population did, in the following fifteen years, increase substantially. Whether or not it was a result of the substantial family allowances we shall never know; however this increase in the population (1949, 41 million; 1968, 50 million), coinciding with an economic policy (under de Gaulle) of maintaining the parity of the franc[1], major expenditure for military and representative ends, and coinciding with an increase in the numbers of older people, produced its own serious problems. There was obviously a shortfall in the social sector (for example, the construction of houses, schools and universities) and the first ominous signs of unemployment (a relatively rare phenomenon in France) – particularly among the young – started to appear. The major manifestation of dis-

[1] During the period 1959–1968 inclusive.

content with the shortfall on the social infrastructure side was evident in the 'May Events' of 1968, whilst the concern of the Government with the rising tide of unemployment (which reached 5% of the labour force at the end of 1970) manifested itself in the wide arsenal of Keynesian measures which were used early 1971. *Tout court*, then, the current problem lies in the structure of the population – an unusually heavy non-working young and old sector, linked with the necessity of encouraging saving in order to improve both the manufacturing and social infrastructure of the country, and linked still further with the necessity of aligning the economy increasingly with those of the other members of the European Economic Community. At all times, the Pompidou Government has one eye over its shoulder, trained on the images of the upheavals of 1968 (hence the measures to placate social demands, continued since the *Accords de Grenelle* of that year), and one eye on their gaullist friends who wish to participate financially to an increasing degree in certain sectors of the economy, for example, telecommunications and road construction. These demands have then caused changes in the planning, fiscal, monetary and anti-cyclical fields of French national economic management. In examining these four different areas, then, we shall note the dual philosophy of gaullist 'market' economy and a continuation (modified, it is true) of French 'dirigisme', demonstrated particularly by the State intervention in regional development. Nowhere is this dual philosophy more manifest than in the Sixth Plan.

1. The Sixth Plan for Economic and Social Development (1970–5)

The Sixth Plan marks a major break with previous Plans. Whereas the Fifth Plan emphasised the qualitative development of the nation, the Sixth Plan, in its introduction to the options of the exercise, comes down firmly on the side of quantity, stressing that there must be quantity before qualitative living can be achieved! Further, the Plan, in its introduction, stresses the virtues of the 'market' economy, thus allowing private enterprise to participate more fully in certain lucrative sectors of the economy (for example, telecommunications and toll-paying trunk roads), thus in turn, making good the shortfall between the revenue and expenditure caused by the exercise.

In order to balance this increased participation in the Plan by the private sector, the State does promise to make a more substantial contribution to the public transport system (for example, in the completion of the central section of the express underground line in the Paris region).

Apart from the usual declamations regarding the nation's military independence, her competitive strength as a trading nation and her duties towards the third world, unusual emphasis is placed on the State's social obligations. Hence, after a relatively long silence on this subject, reference is made to the family and to the necessity of maintaining a large population. (Does this mean even larger family allowances?).[1] In a similar manner, one of the very few references ever made in French planning is made to the necessity of a more just income redistribution. One of the vehicles of income redistribution which is being increasingly used is the old age pension which has recently been increased once again. Here the main objects of the Laroque Report are being realised nine years too late. During the period of the Plan, welfare benefits will increase by between 45 % and 46 %.

Great emphasis is placed on education (the school leaving age will be raised to 16) and to vocational training. Likewise the creation of 250,000 new industrial jobs during the course of the current exercise is stressed. The Plan also categorically rejects even a low level of unemployment. There is at last a serious desire to utilise the influx of young people coming on to the labour market. This is necessary in view of the age structure of France's population – this fact is stressed in the document. Because of this problem, no important reduction in the maximum working week of 54 hours is contemplated, and no reduction in the retirement age is envisaged.

The Plan then sees an average annual growth of between 5·8 % and 6·0 % as being realisable, and accepts price increases of 3·2 % per annum. In view of the emphasis placed on maintaining the parity of the franc in the face of inflationary dangers, it is strange that an incomes policy should be rejected. As is expected, emphasis is placed on saving and investment, and the

[1] Indeed, in the introduction, specific reference is made to increased aid for families with more than two children, and on 28 July, the Government announced that family allowances would be increased by 5·3 % as from 1 August 1971, since when even further increases have been made.

Government promises to find ways of encouraging saving. One of the recent results of this intention has been the publication of the Baumgartner Report on the Paris *Bourse*. This Report forms the subject of a supplement to this chapter.

Thus, in both its emphasis on the attractiveness of a 'market' economy and its detailed reference to social problems and aid, and in its rejection of a 'qualitative' plan (the time not yet being ripe for such a step!), the Sixth Plan marks a major departure from its predecessors, particularly with the Fifth Plan.

2. *Fiscal Reforms*

If the methods of achieving equality and saving, and of preventing unemployment are not particularly clearly set out in the Plan, they have been set out during 1970–1 in three declarations covering fiscal, monetary and anti-cyclical policy. The fiscal aims are fairly ambitious.

The fiscal reforms (set out in 1970) will gradually be introduced over a period of five years, i.e. the period of the Sixth Plan. Despite super-tax being removed in 1971, the main aims of these measures are equality (a better redistribution of income) and increased efficiency in the collection of taxes. Whilst M. Giscard d'Estaing also wishes to eliminate evasion, it is not clear how he intends to achieve this!

Firstly, the total tax receipts. At the moment, direct taxes account for 33% of the total, and indirect taxes for 66%. By 1975 it is hoped that they will be about 40% and 60% respectively. Then, during the course of 1971, the V.A.T. (value added tax) was reformed. Formerly there were four categories whose levels were fixed at 7·5%, 17·6%, 23·0% and 33·3%. By the end of 1971 the two middle categories were fused. Food items were placed in the lowest category, basic products in the central division, and luxury items – for example, sports cars – in the upper category.

Since 1972, in order to improve efficiency in collection, where the contributor agrees, direct taxes are collected on a monthly basis. This is a major change in French fiscal habits.

3. *Monetary Reforms*

The major change which was announced in October 1970 was the decision to abolish direct credit controls in the banking system and to replace them by reserve requirements for both deposits and loans. This was done after it had been found that companies were by-passing the restrictions imposed by the *Banque de France* through direct company-to-company lending. This decision also brings French banking controls more into line with those of other similar nations.[1]

In order to encourage saving, the bank rate was maintained at a high level again in 1971, but was not increased during the course of that summer in an attempt to discourage inflows of 'hot' money.

4. *Anti-Cyclical Policy*

Hitherto we have examined conventional forms of economic management. Apart from the regional incentives contained in the National Plan, the use of Keynesian weapons, due to the relative lack of unemployment in France, has been somewhat rare. However, at the end of 1970, the Government was discreetly informed that the unemployment level was reaching 800,000. Thus an *Opération Jeunes* was introduced whereby the Government would pay firms in twenty-six Departments which took on young people for training over a period ranging from five weeks to six months, half the training costs, salaries and taxes of these young persons. Then, in February 1971, the S.M.I.C. was increased from 3·5 to 3·63 francs per day (an increase greater than the cost of living), and public investment in education and construction was increased up to April 1971. All these measures mark a most important departure from former French practice.

5. *The Baumgartner Report*

This much-awaited Report on the active reform of the Equities Market (the counterpart of the 1963 Lorrain Report on the Bond Market), which had been commissioned in March 1971, was presented to the Finance Minister on 9 July, and made public ten days later.

The main aim of the study was to seek ways of increasing by

---

[1] Due to the heavy influx of 'hot' money into France in summer 1971, obligatory reserve requirements were twice raised, in July and in August, both on loans and on deposits (particularly on current accounts). At the same time, regulations were eased regarding the forward exchange requirements of French businessmen.

50 % the contribution made by the *Bourse* to the savings needed during the course of and for the realisation of the current Plan. This aim falls in line with traditional gaullist thinking regarding the 'market' economy, and the desirability of associating the workers more closely with industry through share-ownership and representation in the running of firms.

The study examines the main characteristics of the French equities market and suggests means of achieving the aim described above.

According to the Report, the French market must be described as 'narrow'. Although the *Bourse* itself is structurally well-endowed, it is narrow in its operations. This is due to several factors. The main one is that French savers tend to place only a small amount (4 %) of their total savings in the form of shares. Then shareholders tend to be old in years and few in numbers. In France, one in thirty-three savers is a shareholder, compared with one in twenty-two in the United Kingdom, and one in seven in the United States of America. The number of institutional savers is small, few foreign issues are quoted on the Paris *Bourse*, whilst the importance of the commercial banks is great.

The main field in which action is suggested is in that of education. The holding of shares must be made more attractive and popular to the general public. One way of doing this would be to extend the broadcast made daily from the *Bourse* at 1 p.m. on television. Then of course the technical and information links between Paris and the provinces should be improved. In order to make shareholding more attractive economically, the taxes on distributed profits should be cut. In a similar vein, reforms in company laws, such as those regarding the nominal value of shares, their classification, the distribution of dividends and liquid capital regulations, are proposed.

The proposals concerning an increased recourse to foreign capital are of considerable interest to anyone studying the evolution of a future European Capital Market. The study, mainly through tax reforms on dividend payments, wishes to make it easier and respectable for foreign investors, particularly institutional ones, to hold French shares. Unfortunately perhaps for the Report, it is doubtful whether this suggestion will be taken up in the near future. Rather it is likely that the export of capital (as was proposed by the French Finance Minister on 3 August 1971) will be facilitated to an increasing degree. However, where this would imply an increase in the purchase of shares in foreign companies by French nationals and the floating of such shares in Paris, this would remedy one of the defects of the narrowness of the French market as described in the Report, and also give Paris an incentive to become again a more important part of the developing European Capital Market, as she was doing until May 1968.[1]

Conclusions

The many changes outlined in this chapter could leave the reader a little perplexed. However, there is a surprising consistence in the policy which has dictated changes in the methods which will be used during the period 1970–5 in the management of France's economy.

Basically, the Plan remains. However, if the Plan, with its emphasis on quantitative growth, improved communications and social equality, is to succeed, then extra savings must be found from somewhere – most obviously (closely in line with gaullist philosophy) – from the private sector. Also the need to bring France into line with the banking practices of her neighbours, linked with the desire to turn Paris into a European Capital Market, and coinciding in a most fortunate manner with inflows of 'hot' money and a balance of payments surplus, are consistent with the aims of the Plan and gaullist philosophy.

What has happened over the past two years reveals a remarkable attitude of flexibility in the management of the nation's affairs. As M. Giscard d'Estaing stated on 3 August 1971, when introducing an important relaxation in the regulations for travel allowances and international monetary transfers, the monetary situation had changed and thus French economic policy would also change.

Will the changes succeed? Obviously the appeal to private funds for the financing of telecommunications and toll-paying trunk road construction is succeeding, largely because it is highly profitable! Whether or not the French savers will turn to the *Bourse* is another matter. They do tend to prefer either

---

[1] See P. Coffey and J. R. Presley, 'London and the Development of a European Capital Market', in *The Bankers' Magazine* (June 1971).

liquid assets or the purchase of luxury apartments. But it is probable that foreign institutional investors will be attracted to Paris – if most of the recommendations contained in the Baumgartner Report are implemented.

As far as the Keynesian anti-cyclical measures are concerned, they seem to have achieved their aim since unemployment has fallen in the country. On this point, though, we should be careful, since some of the upsurge in French economic activity may be largely due to sales of French goods abroad and the influx of tourists into France.

Finally, whilst France still adheres to the gospel of a fixed parity for the franc (and for other European currencies for that matter), this will not be maintained, as was the case during part of the 1960s, at the sacrifice of full employment and a deterioration in the social infrastructure of the country. In the pursuit of this policy, France is fortunate in that the performance of her economy is highly satisfactory in the international field at the present time.

Appendix 1

SPECIAL SOCIAL BENEFITS: *L'ALLOCATION MAJOREE DE 'SALAIRE UNIQUE'* AND *'L'ALLOCATION DE LOGEMENT'*

L'Allocation Majorée de 'Salaire Unique'

Mention has already been made of the special allowances amounting to a maximum of 194 francs per month (introduced on 1 July 1972[1]) for mothers who, desiring to or being forced to go out to work, must pay for someone to look after their children. However the former *allocation de 'salaire unique'* (now increased) also merits some examination.

In some ways this allowance was a complement to the minimum national wage since it was given to modest families which were in receipt of only one wage. A reform of this allowance, in the framework of the family allowances, had already been promised in 1970. At the end of June 1972, the reformed *allocation de 'salaire unique'* was presented to the public. Coming shortly after a governmental declaration that the national minimum wage (the S.M.I.C.) should be raised to 1000 francs per month, as soon as possible, the increased *allocation de 'salaire unique'* did something to calm the waters that had been whipped up by the former announcement.

The increases affected 1,100,000 families[2] with low incomes as from 1 July 1972 and the monthly amount involved was 194·50 francs. Interestingly enough, this allowance is linked with the S.M.I.C. and will increase as the minimum national wage moves upwards. Also of great interest are the provisions made for the award of a special pension for mothers (*Mères de Famille*) who are in receipt of this *allocation de 'salaire unique'*. These pensions will be financed and organised by the family allowance

---

[1] Applicable to 80,000 families at first – a further 20,500 will also be eligible.
[2] Families in receipt of a gross income of 4000 francs per month (taking account of the number of children they have) are automatically disqualified from receiving this allowance.

funds. Increases in the pensions are planned for mothers with large families, thus avoiding any material prejudice in such cases.

L'Allocation de Logement[1]

This is an equally interesting allowance. Formerly it was simply an allowance given to families with modest incomes, allowing them to make up the difference between their resources and the rents demanded. In July 1971 and January 1972, respectively, two bills enlarged the scope of this form of aid, which in its new form became applicable as from 1 July 1972.

The importance of the new measures can be gauged by the increase in the number of persons becoming eligible for such aid – more than a million individuals. Further, the direct housing subsidies in this form will affect 3,500,000 individuals.

In the first place, the bill of July 1971 considerably expanded the number of persons eligible for help, bringing in the aged, the physically infirm and young workers. In the second case, the bill of January 1972, the eligibility was extended to young couples (eligible for the first five years of married life), to couples with only one child and those looking after a sick parent or a physically handicapped close relative.

These changes are particularly important for older people and merit the attention of other European countries. Older people who, forced to move to a different (perhaps recently con- structed) and more expensive home, and unable to pay the increase in rent, will receive the difference between the old and new rents in the form of this allowance. The receipt of this aid will naturally depend upon a number of diverse criteria.

It is possible that these reforms, more than the faltering attempts to encourage worker participation in the management and financing of industry, mark the first concrete steps in the direction of the *Nouvelle Société*, about which so much publicity has been made in France during the past two years.

[1] Originally introduced in 1948.

Table 36

'IMPASSE' BUDGÉTAIRE
(In billion francs)

1961	6·86	
1962	7·06	
1963	6·97	
1964	4·73	
1965	− 0·012	(a surplus)
1966	− 0·006	(a surplus)
1967	− 0·003	(a surplus)
1968	1·941	
1969	6·35	
1970	− 0·005	(a surplus)
1971	− 0·125	(a surplus)

Table 37

SOCIAL SECURITY: DIVISION OF RESOURCES
(As percentage of total)

	Illness and accident	*Family allowances*	*Pensions*	*Unemployment*
1959	27·7	29·4	42·8	0·1
1968	33·9	21·4	44·1	0·6

Table 38

*FAMILY BUDGETS: SOCIAL SECURITY: AVERAGE BENEFITS:
EXCLUDING EDUCATION
(Year 1968)

Annual Income Level	*6,000 F*	*12,000 F*	*20,000 F*	*30,000 F*	*50,000 F*
Bachelor	747	832	908	1,049	1,247
Married no children	1,514	1,657	1,836	2,106	2,486
1 child	1,989	2,075	2,197	2,473	2,910
2 children	5,100	4,967	4,846	5,033	5,623
3 children	8,061	7,815	7,408	7,562	8,150
4 children	10,176	10,003	9,497	9,605	10,160
5 children	12,359	12,145	11,648	11,777	12,412

* For a detailed account see, '*Les Transferts Sociaux*' in *Statistiques et Etudes Financières, 1ᵉʳ Trimestre* (1972/5).

Table 39

NATIONAL BUDGET: ALLOCATION OF NATIONAL RESOURCES
(As percentage of total)

	1965	*1968*	*1971*
Military	22·0	18·8	17·2
Educational and cultural activities	17·8	19·3	21·0
Social	14·1	14·0	16·5
Economic	24·9	28·2	21·8
Housing, regional aids	5·8	3·9	4·8

Table 40

NATIONAL BUDGET AS PERCENTAGE OF G.N.P.

1967	23·48
1968	23·60
1969	24·52
1970	23·36
1971	22·48

Table 41

NATIONAL WEALTH: OWNERSHIP
(Year 1967)

% of population	*% of national wealth owned*
5	40
10	30

(Age group: mainly 45–54)

Table 41A

INCOME DISTRIBUTION: 1971

	Proportion of total population %	Total incomes %
Small and medium wage-earners (80 % of total wage-earners)	62	38
Top salaries	15	29
Fixed incomes (unearned)	23	33

Source: *Responsables* number 34 (1972).

Table 42

MAJOR TRADING PARTNERS, 1971
Major Clients

	% *of exports*
1. Western Germany	21·2
2. Benelux	11·1
3. Italy	10·6
4. U.S.A.	5·7
5. Holland	5·6
6. Switzerland	4·7
7. United Kingdom	4·5
8. Algeria	2·8

Major Exporters

	% *of imports*
1. Western Germany	22·1
2. Benelux	10·6
3. Italy	9·7
4. U.S.A.	9·1
5. Holland	6·1
6. United Kingdom	5·0
7. Switzerland	2·6
8. Sweden	2·2

Source: *Cahiers Français* (January, February 1972).

Table 43

BALANCE OF PAYMENTS 1949–67
(In millions of dollars)

	Goods	Services + Goods	Capital account	Percentage cover of imports by exports
1949	−468	−539	−49	66·8
1950	−78	−115	23	88·1
1951	−771	−970	−24	73·2
1952	−619	−591	102	66·4
1953	−339	282	−9	81·0
1954	−179	−20	−223	86·6
1955	86	272	−179	93·7
1956	−808	−848	−99	72·9
1957	−950	−1,204	345	71·3
1958	−295	−336	511	78·9
1959	436	710	293	99·3
1960	92	643	−49	99·0
1961	417	884	−70	102·8
1962	485	773	−320	98·7
1963	177	384	87	90·9
1964	−89	−22	445	87·9
1965	390	442	112	96·0
1966	−38	−44	12	91·2
1967	150	134	122	90·3

Table 44

BALANCE OF PAYMENTS 1968–71
(In millions of francs)

	1968	1969	1970	1971
Current account balance	−7,184	−10,849	1,307	3,086
Capital movements	−8,448	1,689	4,098	5,240
Courtage international	873	879	1,012	1,649
International settlements	211	−213	41	855
Errors and omissions	−1,293	−1,248	1,166	433
Total	−15,841	−9,742	7,624	11,273

Source: *Ministère de l'Economie et des Finances.*

Appendix 2

Land and Population

Some quantitative comparisons of France with the United Kingdom and Germany may help to put the preceding detailed discussion of France more into perspective. West Germany and the United Kingdom are very similar in land area and population (table (i)), and their overall population densities of over 200 persons per square kilometre are among the highest in the world. France has only a slightly smaller population, but more than twice the land area, so that the population density is under half that of the other two countries. The population is

Table (i)

PEOPLE AND LAND 1970

	Area (000 sq. km.)	*Population* (million)	*Population per sq. km.*	*Estimated population 1980* (million)
West Germany	249	61·5	248	63·5
France	551	50·7	98	54·8
United Kingdom	244	55·7	228	58·9

Source: All tables in this chapter, unless otherwise stated, are taken from *Basic Statistics of the Community* (1972), published by the E.E.C. Commission.

rising in all three countries; already by 1980 there are likely to be two million more West Germans, three million more Britons and four million more Frenchmen. Whereas in West Germany and the United Kingdom some commentators are apprehensive about the effect of more millions on the quality of life, in France population growth is generally welcomed, as tending to increase national influence and economic growth. The French attribute their country's loss of influence, and poor economic performance, in the late nineteenth and early twentieth centuries, to the fairly stable population and, since 1945, have made the encouragement of large families an explicit aim of social policy, as described in the main body of the book.

The geographical distribution of the population differs considerably amongst the three countries. In the United Kingdom and France there is a strong concentration of population in the capital cities (some twelve million in Greater London, some ten million in Greater Paris) with no other urban centre of comparable standing. In West Germany on the other hand there are some six conurbations, all of comparable size, as well as a larger proportion of its population in medium-sized towns of under 500,000.[1]

In the vocational distribution of the labour force, the most striking difference is in the numbers engaged in agriculture, between France and West Germany on the one hand (14% and 9% respectively) and the United Kingdom (3·5%). In both France and West Germany, the agricultural population is falling fast – at the end of the War it was over 20% in both countries – and it will undoubtedly fall further, although probably not to the British level. The larger French agricultural land area alone

Table (ii)

DISTRIBUTION OF LABOUR FORCE BY INDUSTRIES 1970
(000)

	Agriculture	Manufacturing	Services	Unemployed	Total
West Germany	2,406	13,247	11,052	149	26,854
France	2,898	8,321	9,254	356	20,826
United Kingdom	715	11,714	12,475	555	25,459

might be expected to result in a higher agricultural labour force. The main reason for the big difference in agricultural populations on the Continent and in the United Kingdom is that France and Germany did not experience the British enclosure movement in the eighteenth and early nineteenth centuries, which produced relatively large, efficient farms, manned by a smaller labour force. A further reason was the British policy of

[1] For a survey of the problems of London, Paris and the Rhein–Ruhr complex see Peter Hall, *The World Cities* (Weidenfeld & Nicolson, 1966).

free trade – for agricultural as well as industrial products – which prevailed from 1842 to 1931. The competition from cheap foreign foodstuffs caused a contraction and rationalisation of the British agricultural industry which France and Germany avoided by adopting protectionist policies. Since 1945, the countryside of both France and – even more – West Germany has been opened up to the pressures of an industrial economy; the effect has been to drag the agricultural industries of both countries rather violently into the twentieth century. The dilemma is that, whereas a rapid fall in the agricultural labour force is economically desirable, it can cause social disruption and hardship. Both countries have now adopted policies for encouraging the amalgamation of farms, while relieving hardship by means of grants, pensions to retiring farmers, etc.

National Income

The most striking feature of table (iii) is the change in the ranking of national income between 1958 and 1970. In 1958, the United Kingdom had a higher national income (in total and *per capita*) than France or Germany. In 1970, she had been overtaken by both countries, and *per capita* income in Germany

Table (iii)

GROSS NATIONAL PRODUCT AT CURRENT PRICES

	1958 Total ($ million)	1970 Total ($ million)	per capita $
Germany (F.R.)	59,200	186,000	3031
France	53,600	147,600	2911
United Kingdom	64,800	121,400	2179

was nearly 50% higher. These figures – like all international comparisons of national income – need to be treated with caution. They are based on current exchange rates, and do not take account of differences in price levels amongst the three countries. To arrive at an indicator of real income, the figures should be deflated by a price index. This international comparison of price levels is very problematical; it is difficult to obtain representative quotations, and different figures will be obtained according to which consumption pattern is used for weighting. The national income figures probably exaggerate the differences in living standards, but still suggest that the German and French standards are higher than the British.

Table (iv)

AVERAGE ANNUAL GROWTH RATES OF G.N.P. AT CONSTANT PRICES

	Total	*per capita*	*per person employed*
	%	%	%
Germany (F.R.)	4·8	3·7	4·4
France	5·8	4·7	5·1
United Kingdom	2·8	2·2	2·6

Prices

In recent years, average gross wages (at current exchange rates) have been substantially higher in West Germany than in the United Kingdom, whereas those in France have been somewhat lower. There is greater inequality of earnings in France than in Germany, as shown by the fact that in France the top 20% of wage- and salary-earners earn 43% of all earned income, compared with 36% of all earned income in both the United Kingdom and Germany. In addition, the relatively low and unprogressive French income tax means that top salary-earners are very well off indeed. *Changes* in real national income are easier to measure, and here there is no doubt that the growth rates of both France and Germany have been higher than that of the United Kingdom.

Some indicators of material standards of living – and of different patterns of consumption – can be obtained from various physical statistics (tables (v) and (vi)). These suggest less difference in the standard of living than the national income figures (although they also dispose of some of the myths circulated during the Common Market debate, about the Continentals being too poor to afford meat, and having much poorer health services than the United Kingdom). As far as personal impressions are concerned – which are not to be discounted – most observers would probably feel that in West Germany the level of public affluence (theatres, sports facilities, motorways) and private affluence was noticeably higher than in the United Kingdom, but that this could hardly be said of France as regards public affluence.

It should, of course, be added that it is foolish to judge the standard of living by the number of cars, television sets and

Table (v)

FOOD CONSUMPTION 1970
(Kg. per head per year)

	Cereals	Potatoes	Vegetables	Wine (litres)	Meat	Butter	Milk
Germany (F.R.)	66	102	65	16	74	7·2	78
France	78	96	131	108	87	8·2	97
United Kingdom	73	98	62	3	73	7·0	143

refrigerators in a country – particularly if they drive the population to neurosis. (Indeed the excessive preoccupation of some economists with growth has led to a 'backlash' from an equally one-sided 'no-growth' school.) If a country decides to accept a lower growth rate in order to have an easy life, enjoy more leisure etc. that is a thoroughly reasonable choice. But this does not seem to have been the British case. The wage claims recently submitted, and gained, by British trade unions indicate that British workers want a higher material standard of living. The low productivity of British industry is on the whole the result more of inefficiency than of people not working. Hours of work are *not* lower in the United Kingdom than in France or Germany, but anyone who looks around in Britain and Germany must be conscious that efficiency in Britain could so easily be improved without working harder or longer. Moreover whether economic growth is good or bad depends on the use to which it is put. It can be used to produce 'public affluence and public squalor' to quote Professor Galbraith's description of the United States of America in the 1950s, or unprofitable and environmentally damaging projects like Concorde, but it can also be used to produce a more civilised environment. The higher growth rates of France and Germany have at least given them the resources needed for useful public investment, and in Germany the results are particularly evident.

Economists have not achieved much success in giving a purely economic explanation of why different economies grow at different rates.[1] It is becoming increasingly apparent that, often allowing for differences in investment, education etc., the crucial factor is the unexplained 'residual' which can only be

Table (vi)

OTHER INDICATORS OF LIVING STANDARDS

	Crude steel consumption kg. per head	Passenger cars	Motor cycles and mopeds (million)	Telephones (per 1000 population)	Doctors	Hospital beds (per 100,000 population)
Germany	659	13·9	1·3	212	154	1102
France	443	12·5	6·1	161	123	1071
United Kingdom	438	11·8	1·8	153	113	972

a matter of psychological climate and social institutions. In this respect France and West Germany may, ironically, have benefited having started in such a catastrophic situation at the end of the war. Especially in the German case, this necessitated tremendous efforts and a radical re-thinking of policies. Britain, on the other hand, obsessed with her international pretensions – the rôle of sterling, her place in the Commonwealth, the 'special' links with the United States of America and her defence commitments – tended to be complacent about many aspects of her economic and social structure. In addition, neither the franc nor the Deutschmark have been used as a reserve currency, and West Germany has persistently refused to allow her currency to be used for this purpose. Throughout the postwar era, the United Kingdom has tended to invest less than France or Germany (both in public investment such as motorways and in private investment in industrial plant) and to consume more. The figures in Table (vii), showing a lower level of capital investment equivalent to about 17% of G.N.P. are typical for the 1960s.

The lower level of public investment in the United Kingdom

[1] See E. F. Denison and J.-P. Poulier, *Why Growth Rates Differ* (1967).

was the result of decisions by governments. The lower level of investment by businesses is more complex. In some cases, poor performance by an industry can cause it to lose markets, thus reducing the scope for new investment. This has happened to the British motor industry, a typical case being the comparative performance of Vauxhall and Opel. Both are subsidiaries of General Motors, and produce basically similar cars. In the 1950s, Vauxhall produced many times as many cars as Opel, but as a result of consistently poorer detail design, poorer workmanship, and repeated strikes, the position has been reversed, so that Vauxhall now produces only one-quarter the output of Opel, earns much lower profits, and is an unattractive

Table (vii)

USE OF GROSS DOMESTIC PRODUCT 1970

	Private consumption	*Public consumption*	*Capital investment* %	*Balancing item*	*Total*
Germany (F.R.)	54·2	15·8	26·5	3·5	100
France	58·9	12·1	25·8	0·2	100
United Kingdom	62·5	18·3	17·8	1·4	100

competitor for investment from the parent company. British governments have, in recent years, become alarmed at the relatively low rate of industrial investment and have given firms extraordinary generous incentives to invest. But it is doubtful

Table (viii)

WAGE-EARNERS IN MANUFACTURING INDUSTRY 1970

	Average weekly hours	*Average hourly earnings (new pence)*
Germany	39·1	78p
France	44·7	46p
United Kingdom	44·9	65p

whether this is more than treating symptoms. Perhaps a more constructive move would have been to encourage the flow of talent into industry, as in France and Western Germany, rather than into administration and education.

Inflation

In the postwar era, nearly all countries have experienced the problem of a steady, persistent rise in prices. Although the percentage rise each year may seem small, the cumulative effect

Table (ix)

CHANGE IN RETAIL PRICES 1950–70

	Average annual change %	1970 prices (1950 = 100)
Germany (F.R.)	+ 2·3	160
France	+ 4·9	260
United Kingdom	+ 4·1	220

Source: '*Bundesministerium für Wirtschaft und Finanzen*' in *20 Jahre Leistung Zahlen in 1970*, p. 25.

over a number of years produces a very rapid decline in the value of money; for example, at a 3% inflation, the price level doubles in 24 years; at 6% in 12 years; and at 10% in 8 years. These not typical figures are in marked contrast with the experience of the nineteenth century when, in spite of short-term rises and falls, there was virtual price stability from the middle of the century to 1914. Although no country has escaped this 'creeping' inflation, its extent has varied from country to country. In the 1950s it seemed as though West Germany had discovered the secret of (relative) price stability. In that decade the index of retail prices rose, on average, by around 1·5% per annum and wholesale prices remained virtually constant. France on the other hand lurched through recurrent cycles of two-figure inflation, temporarily halted by price freezes before the next bout, while Britain inflated at around 3%, which was widely considered to be a stable and acceptable situation. But in the early 1960s the curve of German price levels began to slope upwards. This acceleration was reduced during the slight German recession of 1966/7 but gathered strength after 1969, rising to 4–5% per annum between 1970 and 1972. In the United Kingdom, there was a similar acceleration after 1968, although from a

higher level; in 1970–2 price rises were running at around 8%
a year. France on the other hand experienced somewhat more
stable prices after de Gaulle's accession to power in 1958; during
the 1960s they were running at an average of around 4% per
annum.

Taxation

In all three countries, the State receives and spends a large
proportion of the national income. The proportion taken in
taxes is markedly higher in the United Kingdom than in the
other two countries, but the proportion taken in social security
contributions is lower. Since compulsory social security contributions are really a form of tax, it makes sense to add them to
taxes. Total government receipts, as a percentage of G.N.P., are
fairly close – 38·6, 38·2 and 40·4 for Germany, France and the
United Kingdom in 1969.

The distribution of tax revenue between indirect taxes
(purchase tax, value added tax), taxes on corporations and taxes
on individuals is fairly similar in Germany and the United
Kingdom, although Germany does not have the very high
British rates on large incomes. The highest marginal rate in
Germany is 56% as against 85% or more in the United Kingdom. The pattern is markedly different in France where the
proportion derived from income tax is lower, and the proportion
derived from indirect taxes higher. The feeling that it is an
imposition to be expected to reveal one's finances to a tax
collector is still strong in France!

Unemployment

All three countries have experienced, for most of the postwar
period, a level of unemployment below the 3% which Lord
Beveridge in 1946 believed to constitute 'full employment'.[1]
The United Kingdom generally experienced rates of under 2%
until 1966 when they rose to over 3%. In Germany, the high
unemployment (7–9%) which emerged after the currency
reform of 1948 was taken up as the economy expanded in the

[1] *Full Employment in a Free Society*. This, admittedly, is taking the official
unemployment figures at their face value. To some extent these may be an
underestimate, since they include people who choose not to claim benefit; to
some extent they may be an over-estimate, since they contain the unemployables.

Table (x)

WAGES, OUTPUT AND COSTS

	Output per man-hour in manufacturing			Hourly earnings in manufacturing			Wage costs per unit of output			Consumer prices		
	Germany	France	United Kingdom	Germany	France	United Kingdom	Germany	France	United Kingdom	Germany	France	United Kingdom
						(1963 = 100)						
1967	126	124	118	132	127	130	105	102	110	111	112	115
1968	137	133	125	138	143	140	101	106	112	113	117	121
1969	144	148	127	151	159	151	104	107	117	115	124	127
1970	147	157	131	170	175	171	115	112	132	120	131	135
1971	153	167	138	190	195	194	124	117	142	127	139	148

Source: *National Institute Economic Review* (May 1972) p. 82.

Table (xi)

GOVERNMENT EXPENDITURE AND RECEIPTS 1969
(% of G.N.P.)

	Expenditure						Receipts			
	Consumption	Investment	Public debt	Current transfers	Capital transfers	Total	Taxes	Social Security contributions	Other	Total
Germany (F.R.)	15·8	3·9	1·0	15·5	1·9	37·4	25·2	10·9	2·5	38·6
France	12·2	3·4	1·2	19·7	1·3	37·5	22·5	14·9	0·8	38·2
United Kingdom	17·9	4·8	4·2	10·8	4·6	41·1	31·0	4·9	4·5	40·4

Table (xii)

BREAKDOWN OF TAX REVENUE 1969

	Total tax revenue (million $)	Indirect taxes	Taxes on corporations (% of total tax revenue)	Taxes on individuals
Germany (F.R.)	38·586	58·1	8·9	33·0
France	31·808	69·8	8·6	21·6
United Kingdom	34·030	55·5	7·8	36·7

early 1950s. Since the late 1950s the German economy – except in the recession of 1966/7 – has been running at less than 1% unemployment (the lowest rate of any country). The number of vacancies has also been higher than the number of unemployed, which suggests that there has been virtually no unemployment,

Table (xiii)

DEMAND FOR LABOUR (UNFILLED VACANCIES MINUS UNEMPLOYED) (Thousands)

	1965	1966	1967	1968	1969	1970	1971
Germany	+ 502	+ 379	– 158	+ 164	+ 586	+ 646	+ 435
France	– 112	– 110	– 164	– 218	– 145	– 167	– 214
United Kingdom	– 43	– 68	– 338	– 353	– 335	– 389	– 614

Source: *National Institute Economic Review*

except of a transitory nature (although the German trade unions do not accept this view). In France, unemployment, although never at the phenomenally low German level, was not a serious problem until around 1970–1 when it began to rise.

External Trade

All three countries are among the world's leading trading nations. West Germany, with 12·3% of world exports in 1970, was second only to the United States of America as an exporter. In third place, at a substantially lower level (6·9%), came the United Kingdom and Japan, with France close behind. These figures include only 'visible' trade (i.e. goods) and exclude 'invisible' imports – commercial services, tourism etc. The United Kingdom earns a substantial surplus on 'invisible' trade, whereas Germany has a deficit (the ubiquitous German tourist, remittances from *Gastarbeiter* etc.). These 'invisible' items, together with capital flows, largely account for the differences in Table (xiv) between the value of exports and imports.

As with exports, West Germany leads in the volume of imports, followed by the United Kingdom and France. Over the postwar period, the most striking changes have been the way in which West Germany has overtaken the United Kingdom as an exporter and importer, and the increased foreign trade of France, which had traditionally been a fairly self-contained economy. France is still more self-sufficient than the United Kingdom or West Germany (as measured by the proportion of exports to G.N.P.) but it has developed exports in fields other than the traditional ones such as wines and foodstuffs, and at the same time acquired tastes for foreign products.

Table (xiv)

EXPORTS AND IMPORTS

	Exports as a percentage of G.N.P. %	Total exports	Total imports
		($ thousand million)	
Germany (F.R.)	18·3	34·2	29·8
France	12·0	17·7	18·9
United Kingdom	16·2	19·3	21·7

Note: This applies only to 'visible' trade

The Environment

Anyone who travels through West Germany is struck by the extensive, and in many ways attractive, rebuilding of its cities. The situation facing the West German cities at the end of the War was incomparably more catastrophic than in France or the United Kingdom. West Germany had not only lost a fifth of its housing stock but also faced an influx of millions of refugees. The subsequent building programme was – in its speed and size – without parallel in history. Although the serious housing shortage has since been overcome, housebuilding has continued at a high level to meet the demand for bigger and better accommodation. The problem of France has been different – a very old housing stock, whose deterioration was aggravated by protracted rent control. More recently, the level of new building has considerably increased.

In the German countryside, the most notable difference from Britain is the large wooded area. Nearly a third of the land area of West Germany is covered by forests, well tended and increasingly used for recreation. France – which covers a much wider range of climate and vegetation than West Germany – also has a high proportion of woodland, although often of a scrub-like

Table (xv)

COMPOSITION OF EXPORTS AND IMPORTS

($ thousand million)

	Imports					Exports				
	Food, beverages and tobacco	Fuels, raw materials	Machinery	Other	Total	Food, beverages and tobacco	Fuels, raw materials	Machinery	Other	Total
Germany (F.R.)	4·9	6·6	5·6	12·7	29·8	1·1	1·9	15·9	15·3	34·2
France	2·4	4·5	4·7	7·3	18·9	2·7	1·4	5·9	7·7	17·7
United Kingdom	4·9	6·5	3·6	7·7	21·7	1·2	1·2	7·9	9·1	19·4

character. The environmental problems of France are more
acute than in the other two countries as a result of the more
recent explosion in uncontrolled speculative building and the
use of hoardings.

Table (xvi)

AGRICULTURAL AND FORESTRY LAND
(1969)

	Wooded area	Agricultural area
	(000 hectares)	
Germany (F.R.)	7,207	13,578
France	12,000	33,127
United Kingdom	1,750	19,368

Table (xvii)

NUMBER OF DWELLINGS COMPLETED 1970

	000	Per 000 inhabitants
Germany	477·9	8·1
France	456·3	9·1
United Kingdom	343·6	6·5

Transport

Although their industrial structures are quite similar, the
transport systems of Germany, France and the United Kingdom
differ in several respects, as a result both of geography and
policy. Both have retained larger rail networks than the United
Kingdom, which carry more passengers, and much more
freight. Both countries have extensively electrified their railways.

These achievements have been at the cost of heavy subsidies;
both countries have, at least implicitly, rejected the 'Beeching'
philosophy that railways should be made to pay or be closed.
In the case of France some branch lines were closed at the end
of the War but were always replaced by excellent bus services

Table (xviii)

TRANSPORT 1970

| | Rail | | | Inland Waterways | | Road | |
	Length of line operated	Passenger-kilometres (million)	Ton-kilometres (million)	Length of waterways in use	Ton-kilometres	Length of motorways (000 km.)	Commercial vehicles in use
	(km.)			(km.)			(000)
Germany (F.R.)	29,694	36,355	71,996	4,353	47,175	4·1	1,201
France	36,981	39,145	70,472	7,526	14,601	1·3	1,900
United Kingdom	19,470	29,612	23,039	603	140	1·1	1,945

and in the field of motor transport Germany was an early constructor of motorways. Britain started motorways construction later thereby avoiding some of the mistakes made by Germany. France, who emphasised rail construction, has only recently started to build motorways. In both France and Germany waterways play a more important role than in the British transport system.

Social Security

Both France and Germany have extensive state systems of social security, which take a higher proportion of national income than in the United Kingdom. Whereas the French system is purely state run, West Germany has an old-established system of private health and pension insurance, which is linked with the state system in a complex way. The German system makes relatively generous provisions for old age, whereas France has relatively high family allowances. Only in Britain does a comprehensive and free national health service exist.

Table (xix)

SOCIAL SECURITY EXPENDITURE AS
A PERCENTAGE OF G.N.P. 1966

	%
Germany	16·0
France	15·5
United Kingdom	12·6

Education

Since the war, all three countries have expanded provisions for education, France in some ways more than Germany. France has developed an almost universal nursery school system, which has not yet been attempted in Germany, and has also given full-time further education to a larger proportion of young people. But in both cases the expansion of further education has run into grave difficulties. In contrast to the United Kingdom, which has, so far, expanded buildings and teachers nearly in proportion to the growth in student numbers, France and Germany have not increased buildings and staff in any comparable way. This is one – although not the only – cause of the violent upheavals in French and German universities.

Note: Statistical Sources

The comparison of statistics from different countries is fraught with pitfalls. It is best to take statistics from international publications, in which statisticians have done their best to ensure comparability. These include publications of the E.E.C. Commission (*Basic Statistics of the Community*), and of the O.E.C.D. (*Main Economic Indicators*). The *Statistisches Handbuch* published by the German Statistical Office also contains a useful international section.

Index